SHATTERED RAPTURES

Lynne Sturrock

Shattered Raptures © 2024 Lynne Sturrock

All Rights Reserved. No part of this book may be reproduced in any form or by any electronic or mechanical means including information storage and retrieval systems, without permission in writing from the author. The only exception is by a reviewer, who may quote short excerpts in a review.

This is a work of non-fiction. The events and conversations in this book have been set down to the best of the author's ability, although some names and details may have been changed to protect the privacy of individuals. Every effort has been made to trace or contact all copyright holders. The publishers will be pleased to make good any omissions or rectify any mistakes brought to their attention at the earliest opportunity.

Printed in Australia

Cover and internal design by Shawline Publishing Group Pty Ltd

Images in this book are copyright approved for Shawline Publishing Group Pty Ltd

First printing: July 2024

Shawline Publishing Group Pty Ltd

www.shawlinepublishing.com.au

Paperback ISBN 978-1-9231-7134-3

eBook ISBN 978-1-9231-7146-6

Hardback ISBN 978-1-9231-7158-9

Distributed by Shawline Distribution and Lightning Source Global

Shawline Publishing Group acknowledges the traditional owners of the land and pays respects to the Elders, past, present and future.

A catalogue record for this work is available from the National Library of Australia

SHATTERED RAPTURES

Lynne Sturrock

Dedication

Dedicated in memory of my beloved sister, Susan (Sue) Briggs, now in Heaven. You inspired me to do my very best in everything but especially in writing and were always there when I needed help or advice.
You are sadly missed but your wisdom remains.

Acknowledgements

Geoffrey Thwaites, my wonderful cousin for whom I am so grateful for believing in me.
Bridie Briggs, my loving niece, who encouraged me to keep on writing.
Dear friends, Heather Haynes OAM and Patricia Humphrey DSJ, for their love and untiring support.

Chapter 1

When SEX Was a Silent and Secret Word

It may be hard for some of you to believe, but when I was a child, I grew up completely innocent of sex and had no idea where babies came from.

Nowadays with sex education, television and computers, young people can easily find out all their questions if their parents don't tell them.

Thank goodness a pregnant lady does not have to hide her baby bump anymore by wearing an unattractive voluminous smock. When I was walking around heavily pregnant, my smock used to make me waddle slightly from side to side. I felt bad enough, without this tent thing making me feel like an elephant.

Today, girls are very lucky and do not have to rush into marriage. Some of you may live with a partner, but in those days, *nice girls* did not dare to do that, as it was known as *'living in sin.'*

It was the custom – if you hadn't already – to announce your engagement at your twenty-first birthday party or you would be known as being *'on the shelf'*. This was a fate that every girl dreaded and so many rushed into marriage to escape being labelled.

However, things have now relaxed and you can *'try before you buy'*.

Oh! How I wish I could have done that!

It would have saved me from being virtually thrown into the deep end on my wedding night with Stan.

Two weeks before the wedding, my sister Sue asked me if there was something wrong.

How well she knew me! She was excited, as she was going to be the bridesmaid and looked divine in her empire line aqua chiffon gown with a bodice of white guipure lace. Mum had gone to a lot of trouble making it and also identical dresses but with puffed sleeves for the two little flower girls, who were Stan's nieces. So after deep thought, I decided to confess in sisterly confidence that I did not know if I was rushing into things. I really wished I could have told her the main reason why I had cold feet but felt it had to be my own private secret.

Sue smiled and said, 'You just have an attack of pre-wedding jitters. Don't worry, Lynnie.'

But I did worry. I wondered why on Earth I was doing this? Did I really love this man?

I certainly did not have the same feelings for him as I had experienced with Joel, my first real love, or even with the teenage crush I had on Malcolm when still at school.

I felt that there was no real chemistry or passionate desire between Stan and me. It was more like a close friendship but I hoped it would blossom into a special kind of love, once we had consummated our marriage.

Of course, in those days, as expected, I was still a virgin and had high expectations of what was going to happen on our wedding night. Being brought up a strict Anglican I believed that marriage was a sacrament of life-long vows, a very serious commitment indeed, and so I thought that being with an experienced man thirteen years older I would have nothing to fear.

Things would somehow be different as he would protect me and I would never be emotionally hurt again. I had had enough of being swept off my feet and was looking for a safe and secure life, as I could not stand my heart to be broken again.

To make matters worse, I had to admit that I still had feelings for Joel, but it was too late to pull out now! Stan and I had had our pre-wedding appointment with the vicar, and Mum and Dad had already spent a lot of money in advance booking the reception and their new outfits. By now, most guests had accepted their wedding invitations and some had already sent gifts!

Eight months before, I had already had my twenty-first birthday party and had not announced an engagement and so

I knew everyone was pleased that I would no longer be *on the shelf*.

'Wow! What a mess!' The only thing I could do now was to try and come to terms with there being no hope ever, for Joel and me, to be a couple. There was no other choice.

I had to go through with the wedding and the sooner the better.

But unfortunately that night, I had a vivid most wonderful dream of when I first met Joel.

Oh! My goodness! What was I going to do now? *Yikes!*

The next day I felt guilt-stricken, as unplanned repeated snippets of my dream kept popping up unexpectedly into my brain.

How could this be happening to me as when I had woken up, I had decided to forget all about it?

However, my dream had suddenly become a nightmare and so my mind quickly responded to my request by making me think of the immediate future.

Sue had arranged a kitchen tea for me with close friends and some of the girls from the insurance office where I had worked in the city. I had already left my job. Stan did not want me to carry on working, as it was the norm for a wife to stay home and be content with household duties. The office staff had generously farewelled me with a very smart table lamp. It was the latest thing, rather than a standard lamp, and I knew I would miss them all so much.

I had momentarily forgotten about the kitchen tea, but the fact was, it was on *tomorrow*!

Mum was planning to make scones, sausage rolls and butterfly cakes – now known as butterfly CUP cakes – and Sue had already bought plenty of McWilliam's Cream Sherry and lemonade for those who didn't drink alcohol. I had offered to help them but they both refused saying that I had enough on my mind. They were so kind and, of course, didn't know of the latest trauma that I had successfully dealt with. So I used this opportunity to busy myself and go through my trousseau.

Stan lived in the house across the road from us with his elderly mother Mildred who was about to move into a granny flat at the home of one her daughters. So everything was really in place for us, except I had bought new bed linen, towels and blankets. Unfortunately, I had recently overheard June from next door telling Mum, *'Stan's a good catch!'* It made me feel uncomfortable for Mildred's sake, having to leave the house she thought was hers without her son. I knew she already didn't like me and three would definitely be a crowd.

I had my Chantilly lace wedding dress, veil and headdress hanging in my wardrobe next to my going away outfit, complete with matching new satin-covered shoes, handbag and gloves. They all looked so glamorous.

Also hanging up was my special wedding night white lace nightie and negligee set. It had been so expensive but I had put it on lay-by with four other different coloured sets and couldn't wait to parade it in front of Stan on our special night.

I had new honeymoon clothes and shoes for day and night and started to feel really excited. The year was 1964 and The Beatles group had just been and left Melbourne after a huge success and stayed at the new Southern Cross Hotel (which is no longer there). It was very popular after that and so I was very lucky to get us a booking on the tenth floor.

Last on the list was my toilet bag complete with a spare box of the pill as I did not want to have a baby until I was ready. I had been too embarrassed to discuss contraception with Stan and was already taking them, as my doctor had advised me to try it for a month before the wedding. It was only new on the market and I had been so self-conscious asking him for it and was amazed when the doctor explained to me how it worked. How I wished that I had had the guts to ask him questions about losing my virginity. I had been so sheltered all my life and was so shy and naïve about these things.

The kitchen tea was great fun for most of the time. I received three toasters and thought I would share them with Mum and Sue. The only problem we had was Jennifer, who had had too much sherry.

'Hope you don't have a tough hymen, Lynne. My husband couldn't get his dick inside me on our wedding night. He was gentle but it took three more nights and then I bled like hell!'

Mum was shocked and came rushing in from the kitchen waving a tea towel in her hand. 'That's enough for today, Jennifer. It's time you all went home. Thank you for coming.'

On that note, all the guests happily left and still stifled giggles, trying not to laugh in front of my poor mother as they bid us farewell.

I thanked Mum for the wonderful party whilst helping her with the washing up and was very careful not to mention Jennifer's unfortunate outburst. It was a shame that I could not ask her something that was worrying me but I did not want to antagonise her anymore.

I went into my bedroom and luckily found Sue in there with all the gifts she had brought in from the lounge room and she was still laughing. My little sister was very clever and studying in her final year at university. She had had all types of interesting part-time jobs in the holidays and so was far more worldly wise, compared to me. She was also keeping company with Harvey, a fellow student who was from America. He was very polite and good-looking and so I decided to bite the bullet and ask her the question. I couldn't ask Mum.

'Sue. Can you please tell me what a hymen is? I didn't understand what Jennifer was talking about before and everyone in the room seemed to know what it was, except me.'

Sue did her best not to express surprise and put on a serious but comforting voice and said, 'The biological meaning is that it is a small thin membrane that surrounds the opening of the vagina.'

At that moment I felt absolutely terrible and burst into tears. 'I don't think I have one. I must be a freak!'

'Oh! Lynnie, every girl has one. It is just you have never looked for it. I suggest you get a torch and a hand mirror. Lie down on the bed and open your legs. To get a good look, use two fingers to part the walls and you will find it at the bottom of your vagina shaped a bit like a half moon. It is very tiny and when you have intercourse with your husband for the first time, it will stretch when his penis penetrates you. Don't worry, just lie back and know that what is happening to you is quite normal. Naturally, you will be nervous the first time and it may be a bit uncomfortable but it gets much better each time and brings you closer together. You will really like it especially when you experience a climax, commonly called COMING! It is an amazing feeling and I should know.'

I suddenly realised that Sue must have *gone all the way* with Harvey. *Yikes!*

'Glad you are on the pill, Lynnie. Single girls like me are not allowed to get a prescription and so Harvey has to use French letters. I have to go now. He is picking me up soon.'

'Thanks, Sue. I love you so much.'

'Love you too, Lynnie. Just forget about what Jennifer said. Her case was most unusual.'

All went well with my little sister's instructions and I finally found that I did have a hymen. Hooray! I was normal! I had really been such an idiot not to find out about these things sooner but how? Also, it explained why I couldn't fit a Meds tampon inside me. I had very painful and heavy periods and was hoping that tampons would give me more freedom as sanitary napkins left a lot to be desired. I had to wear two at the same time for the first three days of my period and it felt like I had a mattress between my legs. I hated it.

Mum had said, 'Even the Queen has periods, and so you just have to get on with life.'

It was years later before the endometriosis disorder was discovered.

However, now I knew what to expect on my wedding night and it wasn't going to be anything to worry about at all. So I naturally thought it would be a piece of cake, for sure.

CHAPTER 2

Wedding Bells

At long last, the great day had arrived.

It was a lovely sunny day in September and I spent the morning at the hairdressers and afterwards had a bubble bath that Sue had given me as a present. Then she helped me get dressed in my wedding dress and fix the veil on my head so that it wouldn't slip off. She was a fantastic help and made me feel so special as she dabbed some of my new French perfume on me.

'You look so beautiful, Lynnie. Good luck and every happiness for the future.' And she winked at me.

'Thank you so much, Sue. You have been so wonderful. I will miss you.' I gazed into our full-length mirror and suddenly realised that I really did look like a bride!

Then I walked into our comfortable, old, antique-furnished lounge room and immediately smelt the familiar, comforting scent of furniture polish. I stopped briefly at various milestone photos of Sue and me proudly displayed on the mantelpiece and crystal cabinet. I found myself wondering how I could ever leave it and start a new life. I was deep in thought when Dad stood up from his favourite chair and amazed Mum and me. He was actually smiling for a change, with raised eyebrows and bright piercing eyes, staring at me and nodding his approval. We were so thrilled.

However, I was starting to feel a bit nervous as Mum and Sue left for the church before us and Dad said, 'What's the matter, Mack?' (He always called me by my nickname when he was in a good mood.) 'Are you feeling a bit queasy in the tummy?'

I nodded and he immediately came to the rescue by giving me a huge dose of a white chalky medicine. Little did I know that it was really used for diarrhoea. 'This always does the trick for me.'

And it did!

I felt like a princess riding in the wedding car with its white ribbons on the bonnet as we drove up to the church. Soon we were inside and ready for Dad to escort me to the altar. I could see Stan standing with the vicar and the others waiting for us. He looked very smart in the latest suit and smiled when he saw me and of course I smiled back and the guests were all so happy for us as we passed by them. It was my day and I had made a decision to make a lasting commitment. Therefore, I was determined to enjoy it, no matter what.

Later on, at the wedding reception, the band played, amongst other songs, 'Fools Rush in Where Angels Fear to Tread' and Gloria, my former singing teacher, caught my eye and looked at me briefly with tears in her eyes. Everyone thought that she was crying tears of joy for me; only I knew she wasn't. She had known all about Joel and couldn't help worrying. However, today he was far from my mind. Thank goodness – I was not on the shelf anymore!

When it was time to go, I changed into my going away suit and we waved goodbye to everyone. Our honeymoon was going to begin on the eleventh floor of the Southern Cross Hotel. They had upgraded us to the top floor and I was so excited as I had never stayed at a big city hotel before. I believed our room had a spectacular view of the city lights and I thought it would be so romantic. I had been looking forward to this night for so long.

When in our room, Stan suddenly surprised me by deciding to have a shower, and so I changed into my white lace nightie and negligee set. It was sure to knock the socks off him. I knew Stan would love it. It was so soft and feminine, and I felt like a film star wearing it.

When Stan appeared from his shower, he was wrapped in a big white towel and without giving me a second glace, he signalled for me to have a shower also. I said, 'I don't need one as I had a long bubble bath at home, just before the wedding.' But he insisted.

Under the shower, I had mixed emotions. Firstly, Stan had not even commented on my beautiful nightie and negligee set. Secondly, he made me feel that I was dirty and needed a wash before we could get close. I thought it was very strange, but then realised that he may be nervous. Of course, I was slightly apprehensive too, but then, I trusted and respected him.

After my shower, I got back into my stunning, white lace outfit, hoping to parade it for Stan as I hoped he would find it irresistible. I was eager to get started and find out what married love-making was all about and what it felt like *to go all the way*. I brushed my long hair smoothly once again, and applied some more Chanel No.5 perfume before stepping back into the bedroom.

Stan was sitting up in bed wearing royal blue and white striped pyjamas and reading a copy of *PIX*, a girlie magazine, with a girl in a brief bikini on the cover. He hardly looked up at me before turning off the bedside lamp. I was speechless! What was wrong? Didn't he want to see me in my beautiful nightie and negligee?

I stumbled into the bed and had to take the negligee off myself. Then Stan lent over and kissed me and asked, 'Are you feeling tired, Lynne, after such a long day?'

I said, 'No, I've had a wonderful day and I am looking forward to ending it beautifully with you.'

Then after several attempts at penetration, Stan stopped and said that he did not want to hurt me and that we would have to try again tomorrow as he had already climaxed. I think that was why I felt an unpleasant sticky warm fluid inside my legs and so wondered why I had had to have the stupid shower in the first place.

My new husband had rolled over and gone to sleep and I was left disappointed, unsatisfied, bewildered and uncomfortable. What had I done? And where were the tissues in this place? I wondered if Gloria had been right in her theory that I had been looking for a father figure. After all, Stan was thirteen years older than me. I went over and over things and reached the conclusion that poor Stan had been nervous and had not wanted to hurt me. I realised that I was very fortunate to have a husband who cared about me and had not taken me by force. There was a whole lifetime ahead of us and so I was determined to make the best of things. As I fell asleep, luckily I managed to put all my negative thoughts of our wedding night right out of my mind but I unfortunately had one terrible thought... *Yikes!*

I hoped I wasn't going to end up like Jennifer!

Chapter 3

Honeymoon Happenings

The next day we set off for the Gold Coast in Stan's new maroon Volkswagen sedan, which was the latest Volkswagen after the old Beetle model. I was looking forward to the warmer weather in Queensland and couldn't wait for our holiday to begin. We left early as we were hoping to stay at the Gypsy Point Hotel near Mallacoota.

Stan had said that it was a delightful little fishing village and very quiet but it had a trick at the pub that often worked. Someone had nailed a two-shilling piece to the floor of the bar and all unsuspecting tourists who tried to pick it up were supposed to shout the locals a free drink, so I had to be careful as we didn't want to fall for it. I laughed and promised to be on the lookout.

The day went smoothly and we were both relaxed. It was great to be alone at last, without any interruptions and just enjoy each other's company. As we motored along, it was late afternoon and we needed a toilet break so Stan stopped at the Orbost Comfort Station and he said that when he had finished, he would drive up the road to the milk bar to get some cigarettes. So I went into the ladies and later on, when I was washing my hands, I heard someone whistling 'Onward Christian Soldiers'. It was coming from over the adjoining wall of the male toilets. I thought it was rather odd to be whistling a hymn but then as I went outside, the whistling broke into singing and I immediately recognised the voice.

It was Joel!

I couldn't believe it! My legs went to jelly and I could hardly breathe.

'What are you doing here, my little cherub?' said Joel.

'I just got married yesterday and I'm on my honeymoon,' I said, shaking all over.

He had always reminded me of Troy Donahue. So handsome with his inviting come-hither wide blue innocent eyes, but now I had ruined my vision of him as he looked crushed and dismayed. 'What did you do that for?'

'You of all people should know,' I snapped and was on the verge of tears. 'I thought you were happy when you decided to join the Bush Brotherhood, so far away in Katherine, in a remote part of the Northern Territory. So, it is more like, *why are you here, Joel?*'

'Unfortunately, Lynne, I found that being a Bush Brother Missionary was not for me and I couldn't face having to be celibate for the rest of my life. I had to find out if it was my true calling from God and after nearly finishing my training, I realised that it wasn't. I still want to be a priest in a suburban parish. I have just arrived home and wanted to see you but thought I should see my parents in Mallacoota first. It's amazing that we have just run into each other like this isn't it?'

I agreed but before we could finish our conversation, Stan's car appeared and I warned Joel that Stan was very possessive. So he left reluctantly, looking down at the ground, obviously disturbed and I think he knew he had missed the bus.

Stan was furious when he pulled up and asked me who the man was that I was talking to, thinking it was a stranger, making a nuisance of himself. I said that there was nothing to worry about as he was an old friend who used to be our curate at my church – the *Reverend Joel Peterson*. However, Stan was like a dog at a bone and would not let it go until he had found out if Joel had been my boyfriend. I kept on protesting that it was years ago and had just been a crush and that I would have married Joel if it had been serious and not him.

He cooled down then and thank goodness, it seemed to make him feel better.

Very soon we were on our way again and had begun to talk about other things, although in my mind I was still absolutely flabbergasted. It was a strange coincidence running into Joel on my honeymoon miles away from Melbourne, at a toilet block!

It was all too incredible, to be true but I had to take control of myself as my feelings for Joel were starting to resurface.

Twilight had come and we turned off the main highway at Genoa and continued along a single lane road to the Coast but a car had kept following us for ages and made no attempt to pass us. Stan started getting impatient and put his foot down on the accelerator but still the car kept on our tail. Finally, he had had enough and asked me to turn around and see what was going on. Even though it was dark, Joel saw me and immediately gave me a secret wave and then I felt as if I was in the middle of an explosive situation as I confessed to Stan who it was.

By this time, Stan was very annoyed and slowed right down. Then it was Joel's turn to accelerate and he sped past us. After the next few miles, we could see no sign of his tail lights, which was a welcome relief. However, just before the turn off to Gypsy Point or Mallacoota, we saw a car stopped at the cross roads with its lights flashing on and off. It was Joel's car and I asked Stan to stop as I thought that something must be wrong. However, he chose to turn back and did not stop until we had driven all the way back again to Genoa. I didn't know what to think.

Why had Joel done this?

But I never found out as I never saw him, ever again.

After a quiet dinner at the motel, we started to settle down and enjoy ourselves. This time, I was ready for a shower before bed and so chose to have it first. I changed into a black nightie and negligee but I still could not forget Joel. The feelings I still had for him were pouring out of me but I was determined to do the right thing and be a good wife to my husband. Stan loved the black outfit and started kissing me with new determination.

Meanwhile, I was already warmed up with thoughts of Joel and didn't even care when Stan entered me early as I was ready. The ecstasy that followed felt wonderful and Stan whispered that he loved me. We both lay close to each other for quite a while before we felt like moving. I had really been on fire and now I knew what this part of marriage was all about.

I had learnt from the night before to have tissues on hand and that I had to warm up quickly as for some reason Stan was always in a hurry. I thought it was because he loved me so much but of course, I had never heard of foreplay, premature ejaculation or orgasms. I only knew that I had experienced my first climax and had given it the thumbs up. It seemed good every night after that and all I had to do was imagine that I was with Joel and it just happened. I became excited very quickly and so did not miss out on having a climax. Of course, I was hoping that in time I would forget about Joel and that my sexual urges would all be transferred to Stan. At that point in time, I realised that I really did love Stan but part of me still loved Joel.

Yikes! If only we hadn't run into each other at Orbost. On the other hand, seeing him again had brought back all my feelings for him, which had helped me to accelerate my sexual desire, when I fantasised about him. I hated having to do it, but it was the only way I could be aroused quickly. With Stan always in a rush, I knew that I had to work fast so that I could be satisfied as well. It was all a bit disappointing but I was certain things would work out somehow. Surely, my memory of Joel would diminish one day soon and then I would only think of my husband as my true love, which now I really wanted.

When our honeymoon in Surfers Paradise was drawing to a close on the last morning, we went for a walk along Cavell Avenue and I saw a tourist bus stopped at the traffic lights. We were on the other side of the road but there was someone waving to me frantically from an open window. It happened to be Nola Jenkins – a friend from work – and I rushed over.

'How is your honeymoon going, Lynne? We have all been thinking of you at the office?'

'It's been absolutely fabulous!' I shouted as the bus moved away and I really meant it.

Then Stan said jokingly to me, 'I'm glad that wasn't one of your crazy boyfriends!

Chapter 4

Married Life

We survived the honeymoon and at last arrived back home in Mount Waverley. Stan had taken a long and tedious inland road, far away from Orbost and Mallacoota and I found it quite daunting to be going home to Stan's house across the road and not to my family's home.

Stan went back to work selling new home and land packages immediately and I hardly saw him as he said that his main ambition was to be a millionaire by the time he was forty and he only had a bit over five years left to achieve it. I, on the other hand, was at a real loose end as not being allowed to return to my job or continue with my singing lessons, or any church activities.

I felt really awful because Mum was still working and there was I, so much younger at just twenty-two, home all day. To make matters worse, I soon started feeling that I was living in a gold fish bowl as the neighbours beside me and at the back took great delight in gluing themselves to their windows and watching my every move, especially when I was pegging out all my pretty lacy night wear and lingerie washing on the Hills Hoist clothesline.

The neighbours were Mum and Dad's age, and so I had nothing in common with them. It really was a shame that I had no car as I felt locked in all day and really bored. The only consolation I had was that I loved the convenience of being close to my family. Unfortunately, though, the only time that they were at home was mostly when Stan was at home and he got upset because in his opinion, I was always over there and neglecting him.

To top it off, Mildred did not want to come and visit us, as she still called *our* home, *her* home. So we decided to move in a hurry and luckily found a brand new house on Oliver's Hill in Frankston. I loved it because it had a glimpse of Port Phillip Bay from the front porch but the annoying thing for me was that it had no telephone connection and it would not be available for a long time as it was a new estate. Thank goodness that the nearby milk bar had a public red phone inside their shop for customers and I made good use of it.

Two weeks after we moved in, I received a letter from St Andrews Private Hospital in Melbourne giving me a date for an operation in a few days to remove a cancerous mixed parotid tumour. I really trusted my lovely surgeon, Mr Campbell, but all the same, I could not help feeling very nervous when he had warned me that if his scalpel slipped, the whole of the left side of my face would drop and I would be disfigured for life. He had put the operation off until after the wedding and honeymoon were over as he knew I would not want a recent scar from stitches to show up in the photos.

When the day came for the procedure, Stan was busy and so dear Mum came out of her way to collect me and admit me to the hospital. She was a great support but also nervous, like me.

We need not have worried though, as when I woke up, the operation had been successful and Mr Campbell said, 'You have been such a good patient, pet. You won't even have a scar left after it all heals, as I was very careful. Now, all you have to do is get better and get that new husband of yours to look after you for the next week or so.'

He gave me the name of one of his friends, a local doctor from Mornington, in case I had any problems before my next appointment to see him in a few days. As he left, he smiled and squeezed the toes of my foot through the covers. He was such a nice man and I wondered what his friend, Dr Stewart Applegate, would be like. As it happened, I had needed to find a new local doctor and I had run out of birth control tablets. Stan kept forgetting to get them as we had no chemist nearby and had now confessed he had lost the repeat prescription.

I had been sharing a twin room with Joyce, a dear old lady in the next bed and she loved watching me wearing all my trousseau nighties and negligees. She said that she thought it was sad that I had to be separated from my husband so soon after my wedding. I was quite surprised then, to realise I wasn't really missing Stan very much really. He had not been to visit me at all as he had been too busy working but then Mum, who was working at her boutique on Toorak Road and Sue, who was at Monash University, had both called in twice.

However, I was due to be picked up by Stan that night and it would be so good to get home and have a peaceful sleep as the hospital was so noisy, even at night.

A few days before the operation, I had had plenty of time to think about our future and tried to be optimistic. At least we had a 'sex life', even though it was just one big rush. I had secretly sent away for a book, which had just come on to the market. It was about the sexual enlightenment of women and it discussed all sorts of things about subjects that I had never thought existed, including premature ejaculation, foreplay, mismatched libidos in partners and nymphomania. Unfortunately, now I knew that I would just have to put up with Stan's premature ejaculation, but I dared not discuss it with him as I knew that his pride would not let him seek help from a doctor. I just wondered how long it was going to take to right itself or if it ever would. Another thing that puzzled me was that even though I managed to have an orgasm, each time, I still felt that there should be something more. It reminded me of the Peggy Lee song 'Is That All There Is?', but I hadn't finished reading the book, which was hidden at home. Thank goodness, I still had strong fantasies of Joel to help me through it all.

At this moment, I had to concentrate on recovering from the operation and the last thing I needed to worry about was sex.

Stan dutifully arrived that evening at the hospital to take me home and was happy to see me but I had to warn him that the doctor had said I was very fragile and so to be gentle with his hug and kiss. Joyce nodded her approval and said how wonderful it was that I had such a lovely man to take care of me. She was smiling but I noticed a tear in her eye as we left.

It was a long way from the city to Frankston and halfway home, I suddenly felt that I needed a painkiller. I could not speak properly as my left jaw was still stitched tight and moving my head from side to side was out of the question so I told Stan with great difficulty. He said that he had put my beauty case in the boot of the car and couldn't I wait until we were home? I gave in as I just wanted to get there as quickly as possible.

When we pulled up outside the house, I got out of the car slowly and carefully, as Stan was putting the car away in the garage, and I was left to negotiate the steep front steps. It took me all my strength to make it up to the front door. I took one step gingerly at a time and wearily counted the thirteen of them, and was so glad to get inside. I made my way to the kitchen to get a glass of water for the tablets and was confronted with stacks of dishes and glasses, piled high on the sink and benches and empty beer bottles on the floor. My new kitchen looked like a pigsty. After what seemed like an age, Stan came in with my bags and said, 'What's for tea tonight?'

I couldn't believe that he thought I was in a fit state to be cooking dinner for him. I mumbled that I needed to take my medication and go straight to bed as the pain had now become worse. I rinsed out a glass and filled it with water and found my tablets and headed for the bedroom. As I went down the passage, I had to step over articles of clothing that it seemed Stan had just stepped out of and left all over the floor. It looked like his whole wardrobe was lying there, waiting for me to pick it up and wash it. Even our bed looked a mess. Of course, the sheets had not been changed since I had left and I could tell it had not been made either. I noticed there was cigarette ash everywhere from overflowing ashtrays on Stan's bedside table. It was not the welcome home I had expected but I was in so much pain and discomfort that I was past caring and was just so thankful to get into bed.

I suggested that Stan go out and buy Chinese takeaway and he impatiently said that he had already had it twice during the week. So I said that he could get whatever kind of food that he liked as long as there was something for me that did not have to be chewed. He walked out in a huff, saying that he was upset that he was not getting a home-cooked meal from his wife and left the house, slamming the front door.

In the meantime, I settled down, trying to let the pain killer work. It had never occurred to me that Stan could not cook, wash dishes or his own clothes, but then I realised that his mother had waited on him hand and foot for his whole life. It was now obvious why he had relied on takeaways and not on the fridge and freezer full of food that I had left for him.

When Stan returned, I was feeling a bit better and was looking forward to my meal. Unfortunately for me, it was all food that had to be chewed so I ended up getting out of bed and warming up some tomato soup from the pantry for myself. Stan was furious, saying, 'If you could do that, then you should have been able to cook for me.'

He had missed the point. I was just out of hospital and I was the one that needed looking after, not him.

By this time, I was so tired and exhausted that all I wanted to do was go to sleep.

Suddenly, Stan came into the bedroom after apparently drinking copious glasses of beer and made an announcement.

'Tonight, we are going to start a family! I've waited long enough!'

I was so shocked and objected as strongly as my voice would allow.

'Oh. No! Not tonight, Stan! No!'

How could he think of such a thing when I was like this?

'I missed you so much when you were away. I could have lost you in the operation. If you had died, then I would have been left alone with no children.'

I couldn't believe what I had just heard.

Was that all he thought of me? Some kind of baby machine?

What occurred next was a heartless, frenzied attack on a helpless victim.

I had never heard of rape within marriage before but unfortunately, I had just experienced it.

Chapter 5

Life Goes On

After a few days, Mum drove me into the city to see Mr Campbell to get my stitches out. I was so thankful when he said, 'Everything went well, Lynne. The mixed parotid tumour was a slow-growing malignancy but if it had not been removed, you would have died in eight years. Don't be alarmed. I think I got it all but it is important to keep a watch on the spot, just in case it ever starts to grow again. If one tiny cell has been left behind, it could develop into a tumour again. The chance is remote but all the same, it is my duty to let you know.'

The subject changed when I showed him my wedding photos that he had been eager to see. He smiled at Mum and complimented her on having such an attractive daughter. Then he said to me, 'You made a beautiful bride, pet. That husband of yours is a very lucky man.'

But I didn't even care about Stan, or the wedding photos, any more. I had lost all respect for my husband and felt as if I was caught in some kind of trap. As we were leaving, Mr Campbell reminded me about his colleague, Dr Applegate, whom he said, if I liked, would look after me from now on. On the way home, Mum and I both agreed that I had been very fortunate in having such a gifted surgeon and also one who was so caring and down to Earth.

Since the night I had come home from hospital, I was grateful that Stan had not wanted to make love since then as I wasn't ready for it. He appeared to be very remorseful and sorry for what he had done but he had neglected the most important thing, which was, of course, *to tell me!* However, I decided to go and see Dr Applegate and get a new prescription for the pill, for six months, as I wanted to be prepared for when we did have sex again.

The moment I saw Dr Applegate, I liked him. He was very charismatic and had bewitching blue eyes and an enchanting, mischievous English accent. I found him easy to talk to, as he was so friendly. He had a great sense of humour and I found myself laughing all the time and he said that all his patients called him Stewart and so I said he could call me Lynne.

However, before writing my prescription, he became serious and asked me when I had had my last period. Normally I was as regular as clockwork but this time it was well overdue and so he suggested that an internal examination would be necessary. I didn't like the sound of it as I had never had one before but he was very gentle and kind. After he had finished, he said, 'I've got something wonderful to tell you, Lynne. You are pregnant!'

I was stunned!

How could this have happened? We had not been intimate for weeks.

It was then I realised that the night I had come home after my operation, when I was forced to have sex against my will, I must have conceived. I had run out of the pill before I went into hospital and of course, Stan had lost the darned prescription.

I had been unprotected on that fateful night, and Stan must have known that.

I was close to tears and felt let down once again by my husband and then Stewart said, 'You don't seem to be very happy about this, Lynne. Was this by chance or an unplanned pregnancy?'

'It was definitely not planned by me!' I said, wiping some tears away.

'Would it make you feel better to talk about it?' said Stewart. 'You can tell me anything, you know.'

I nodded and then told him, 'We have only been married a short time and so I did not want to have any children yet.'

After all, I had just had enough on my plate for the time being as I was only just coming to terms with the fact that I was alive and well after my operation. I had not considered myself ready just now to take on such a huge responsibility.

In my mind, I thought there was plenty of time to have a baby but my husband, Stan, seemed to think differently. He had come from a country family of ten children. His father had had two wives. The first wife, Eileen, died in childbirth after having six children and the second wife, Mildred, Stan's mother, had four children and Stan was the second last.

'Is Stan's family Catholic?' said Stewart and I shook my head.

'No, they are Methodists.'

'Well, is there anything else you wish to tell me?' he said, sneaking a look at his watch.

'Yes,' I whispered and I caved in, telling him about the rape. He was visibly shocked.

'Don't worry, Lynne. I will help you through all of this. You are not alone.' Then he led me to the doorway and said, 'Come and see me next week, and let me know how you get on telling your husband the good news. Good luck!' He gave my upper arm a short squeeze, just after saying goodbye to me. Then we both looked at each other and smiled. I felt so good and completely relaxed as if a weight had been lifted from my mind and I seemed to float out of the surgery. What a relief! At last, I had found someone in whom I could totally trust and confide in. Stewart had been amazing.

Stan was thrilled to hear that I was pregnant and so was everyone else, and that included me! It had now hit me and it was wonderful as Stewart had said. Suddenly, I had become very excited about it and aware that now, more than ever, I had to make our marriage work. So I started to be just what Stan wanted. I became a carbon copy of his mother, picking up after him, cooking, cleaning and asking before every meal what he preferred. I seemed to be having a very boring and mundane existence but I was determined to do it.

After all, right now, I had a baby to think of.

Chapter 6

Our Bundle of Joy

Before long, I was suffering severe morning sickness at all hours of the day and Stewart said to carry a bottle of Dexsal Antacid wherever I went as it could help and not harm the baby. I was also feeling quite lonely just doing my housewifely duties and decided to write a letter to the telephone company asking for a phone, seeing I was pregnant, and *hooray*, one was connected in five days. Stan was amazed and I actually got a pat on the back from him.

The next Sunday, Mum and Sue came down to see me. We had a lovely time catching up and I felt almost back to normal again. Sue had great delight in relating her latest stories of her various jobs during the last university holidays. She had us enthralled.

'I started in a peanut factory,' she said, 'but I soon found out that I was allergic to the dust from the shells and had endless fits of sneezing all day and, as you know, I suffer from asthma, which did not help. So next, I tried working in an electrical factory, putting a part into electric eggbeaters as they came along on a conveyor belt. But I came home with head and neck aches, so that job did not last either. My favourite one was selling Diner's Club memberships.'

Then Mum chipped in and said, 'I hardly recognised her, Lynnie, when I happened to be walking in that part of town after attending a buying trip for next season's fashions. Sue was wearing a beautiful blue and gold uniform and it complemented her blond hair, which she wore in a French roll. She was sitting in a blue velvet curtained kiosk outside the Grosvenor Theatre in Little Collins Street and I saw her give out Diner's Club membership application forms to prospective members and I was so proud of her.'

But Sue said, 'It was sad when poor homeless men got the wrong idea from the signs and asked for free dinners. However, when the promotion finished, the manager of the cinema employed me as a part-time usherette and I really enjoy that now, and I get to wear another smart uniform. It is quite safe for all the ladies who work there, as our boss Mr Fisher, keeps a gun in his office drawer in case we get held up. Of course, when Mum heard that, she had a fit and said, "As far as I'm concerned, Susan, you will not be going back there, ever again!"'

Sue and I stifled our giggles and it was just like old times again.

Meanwhile, Stan was becoming more ambitious by the minute in achieving his millionaire goal and so having a home phone helped him with his after-hours business calls. It wasn't long before he and three other workmates formed a company of their own. It specialised in land development. The aim was to purchase broad acres, subdivide the land into building blocks and then sell them off. As the meetings were mainly at our house, I sat in on them and became involved. My suggestion of a name for the company, Terra Firma Proprietary Limited, was unanimously adopted. I felt, at last, I had a purpose, other than being a barefoot and pregnant housewife.

I used to spend the whole week scanning the papers for land advertised that I thought may be suitable, which had existing road frontages, and all the men were very impressed with what I found. Stan was happy that I was interested in his venture and the quality of my contribution but I could tell he resented any extra little bit of attention the other men gave me, so I had to be very careful. I didn't want to do anything to rock the boat at this stage as I was trying my hardest to be a good wife to my husband, even though it was clear to me that I was not in love with him.

However, deep down, I was hoping in my heart that when the baby came, I would feel differently about him. After all, he was the father of my unborn child and I still believed in miracles. Stan was so anxious to step up the ladder in his career that he applied for, and got, a new, better-paid job. It was sales manager of one of the largest home-building companies in Melbourne. It was a feather in his cap but also very demanding and stressful. Although he was getting home later and later every night, he seemed to thrive on pressure and had a sign on our bathroom mirror, which read:

One million pounds before I'm forty.

On the 18th November 1965, dear little Paul Stanley came into the world, after a very long labour. He looked absolutely beautiful with sky-blue eyes and wispy fair curls. He was like an angel and I loved him instantly. I was exhausted after the extremely painful long labour and my stitches were very sore but I didn't care. I had had a son and from the look on Stan's face, a few hours later, I had done the right thing and everything was going to be all right from now on. The joy that the baby had given me had brought back the love that I once had for Stan.

All the bad memories in the past seemed to have been erased. It was incredible.

My only regret about the birth was that Stewart had not been there for it. He had explained the week before that he would be on holidays but as he was not going away, he said he would come for me if the hospital rang him. Unfortunately, the nurse on duty was very unco-operative and insisted I have the locum doctor instead. Also, Stan had decided earlier that he did not want to be present at the birth and so I felt very alone during the horrendous labour.

Mum and Sue managed to find the time to come and visit me the next day, and Mum said, 'I have never seen a more perfect-looking baby.' Also, Sue was thrilled to be an auntie and Mum was delighted to be a very young grandmother. However, as they were about to leave, Mum said that she was very sorry that she could not stay to help me with the new baby when I went home. She explained that even though Sue was still living with them, Dad said he needed her to look after him as he could not manage without her, even for a few days.

Poor Mum! She could not be in two places at once and was torn between her loyalties.

Unfortunately, someone had to miss out and in this case, unfortunately, it happened to be me.

Chapter 7

Can Leopards Ever Change Their Spots?

I arrived home to a clean tidy house as I had made it very clear that I did not want a repeat episode of last time when I returned home from hospital. This time, Stan had stayed with one of his sisters, thank goodness, so the house was just as I had left it, which made me feel so glad to be home with our dear little son, Paul.

I breastfed Paul for ten weeks and that was an enormous strain. He was not a contented baby but it wasn't for the lack of milk. My poor huge breasts were nearly at exploding point before each feed and he did not suffer from colic. I didn't know what was wrong, but the district nurse who came to visit said that he would grow out of it the older he got. Unfortunately, I was not getting any proper sleep as Paul was not sleeping through the night or the day for longer than three hours at a time. I had cloth nappies to wash and hang out to dry and Stan's shirts to wash, dry and iron, and of course, meals to prepare and a house to clean. I was exhausted!

Stan was engrossed in his new job and was no help to me at all. In fact, he was becoming very nervy and said that the baby was keeping him awake at night, so he started drinking more to make himself sleep better. It was quite alarming because he would come home late at night inebriated after driving a long way from his head office at Mulgrave and was finding it difficult to climb up the front steps.

I was at my wit's end. I knew Stan was doing all of this for Paul and me, so I decided to go and see Stewart and tell him what was happening. He was very understanding and said, 'In my opinion, you have given Paul a head start and it is time to get him on to the bottle and have one of your family come down for a day and let you sleep undisturbed for the whole day.' Then he gave Paul a full examination and said, 'It is very puzzling. There is nothing physically wrong with him and he is such a beautiful-looking baby, just like his mother! Please let me know how you go.' He was such a nice man, very similar to Mr Campbell.

The little bit of respite I had from Mum and Sue coming down one Sunday really was like heaven! They took one look at me and sent me to bed as they knew that I was in a bad way. I felt like a new person when I woke up and to my delight, all the household chores were done, Paul was bathed, fed and asleep, and dinner was on the table. I loved them so much.

Even though I had temporarily caught up with everything, Paul continued to cry endlessly, night after night and day after day. When I thought I could not stand it anymore, the Baby Health Centre nurse said it was time to start Paul on solids at six months. This made a lot of difference and he was now sometimes sleeping six hours a night but he still cried a lot when he was awake. Other mothers at the Health Centre didn't seem to be having this trouble with their babies and I couldn't help experiencing a gut feeling that something was not quite right.

When I was pregnant, I made friends with three other 'mums to be' who were at the anti-natal classes at the hospital with me. We found that we all lived quite close by and had our babies around about the same time so I kept in touch. When our babies were about four months old, I decided to invite them over to my place for afternoon tea. I hoped that Paul would not cry too much but unfortunately, this was not the case. He bawled all the time. I could see by the looks on my friends' faces, that they thought it was my fault. I opened up and told them that what they were witnessing was normal behaviour for Paul. They were concerned and sympathetic, and asked obvious questions. I told them that Dr Applegate couldn't find anything wrong with him. Throughout the afternoon, I noticed that their babies were far more advanced than Paul and enjoyed being propped up in a sitting position. They also liked looking and smiling at people but Paul was not up to that and had never had direct eye contact, even with me.

He just lay down in his cot and screamed, no matter what we did. Everyone tried to be supportive and helpful but it was clear that they had enough to think of with their own babies without getting involved in my problems. It was understandable that none of them ever invited me back to their houses but it was devastating and so deflating for me. I felt like the neighbourhood outcast and had lost the only new friends I had made.

As Paul became older, his incessant crying started turning into a constant kind of loud monotone moan, and that was something that I had to learn to live with on and off for twenty-four hours a day. Stan refused to help me and said, 'I'm too busy making a future for us.' He only came home to eat and sleep and it seemed that he was distancing himself from us. However, one day, Paul sat up and I was so relieved. I told myself that he was just a little bit slower than other children his age and most likely would advance as time went on

When it was Paul's first birthday, Sue and Mum invited me home to Mount Waverley for a little birthday party for him one Sunday. Mum had most kindly given me her old Morris Minor when she bought herself a new car as Stan had said he didn't have enough money to buy me one. I had needed a car desperately so that I could transport Paul around safely and so once more, Mum had saved my bacon. That day she had gone to a lot of trouble making a birthday cake for Paul and had cooked us a lamb roast. Sue had bought him lots of presents and we had a happy time taking photos. Just before our lunch, I put Paul down for a nap and crossed my fingers that he would settle down and doze off. As we sat down to eat, Paul started crying non-stop and it was so loud that we could not hear each other speak, even though he was in a bedroom at the end of the passage.

Dad was livid and said, 'How can Stan let his son behave so badly?'

I tried to tell him that that was the way Paul was and that I really did not know how to deal with it and neither did Dr Applegate. Mum suggested that now Paul was one year old, I should go back to the doctor and have him referred to a paediatrician. We continued our meal and tried to carry on a normal conversation with great difficulty. Then Dad asked, 'Is this the sort of thing happening every day? I cannot stand it!'

I said that it did but assured him that I was getting used to it. I could tell that no one believed me. I had dark rings under my eyes and was so tired that I kept yawning all the time.

'What Paul needs is a man's strong influence as your good-for-nothing husband is never there to be a proper father to him.' Finally, as the screams got worse, Dad said, 'I will go and try to pacify him.'

This surprised us as it was well known that Dad had a short fuse. He went along to the bedroom but I had reservations.

I knew what Dad was like and I hoped that he was not going to get the razor strop out, that he used to belt me with when I was two years old being toilet trained. But amazingly, little Paul's cries stopped almost immediately and we all thought that Dad was some kind of genius. Then shortly after, we heard them again and then there was silence. Sue had to go to the toilet at that time and after a while, she came back to the table carrying Paul, who was unbelievably quiet, considering his mood before. She put him in his high chair and gave him a Teddy Bear Biscuit. I was so pleased that Dad seemed to understand my predicament and had been willing to help but suddenly, it seemed the birthday party was over when Sue announced it was time for Paul and I to go home and followed us out to the car. She looked very serious and spoke quite softly, and told me what she had seen happening before in the bedroom. 'I'm sorry, Lynnie, but I caught our father trying to suffocate Paul with a pillow.'

I was so shocked that I vomited in the gutter and we both cried.

CHAPTER 8

New Nightmares

I heeded Mum's advice and took Paul back to see Stewart for a referral to a paediatrician.

Stewart agreed that it was a good idea as there appeared to be nothing physically wrong with Paul. Then I decided to mention that I had never had any real eye contact with him. So Stewart immediately clapped his hands behind Paul and he did not respond. He called his name and then asked me to do the same but there was still no response. However, he did respond when the internal telephone buzzed. Then Stewart said, 'Before we do anything else, I think we should have him tested for hearing at the Commonwealth Acoustics Laboratory, just to make sure that he isn't deaf or partially deaf.'

Stan was outraged that such a test could be even considered. He said that there had never been anyone in his family that had been deaf and that Applegate was clutching at straws. However, later, he did relent but as he was too busy to come, it was left up to Mum and me to take Paul for his test. It was quite a long morning as we had to go into the city. After a physical examination of Paul's ears, we were taken to a room that had speakers placed at different heights and in different directions. Then a series of sounds were played, such as a baby crying, a car driving by or birds twittering. It was puzzling as he ignored most of them but responded to some. The doctor concluded that Paul was not deaf. He had selective hearing, which meant that he only responded to sounds when he wanted to. I was so relieved that he wasn't deaf as I knew that Stan would never have been able to accept it.

But as we still didn't have a reason for Paul's behaviour, Stewart referred us to the paediatrician. Unfortunately, the visit proved to be fruitless and baffled the doctor completely. However, I was given a prescription for a sleeping medication for Paul as the doctor could see that I needed proper sleep badly and so that was a great help to me.

A few weeks later, Sue came to see me as she had been very worried about what had occurred during Paul's birthday party and how I was going. We had decided not to tell Mum about it as we knew it would have been too much for her to bear. The main thing was that Dad knew that we knew and we felt that that was enough. However, it did not excuse his violent behaviour and we both wondered why he had this dark side to his personality.

Then Sue started telling me about Dad's latest outburst. 'Last night I was a bit slow in getting into the house and we were parked outside in Harvey's new sports car when Dad happened to come out with the milk bottles clinking madly and caught us canoodling. He gave poor Harvey a threatening stare and ordered me to hurry up and get inside. Then as I walked up on to the front porch, I heard him shout out madly to Harvey. "You were lucky you weren't called up to go to Vietnam! Kids like you wouldn't know what hit them in the armed forces! No flash cars and no cushy life over there. Of course, I had to do my bit for the country. I had to go to the Second World War and was in the Royal Australian Air Force!"'

We both had a giggle but perhaps this was a part of the puzzle that had made him how he was.

When Paul was nearly two, he was still not walking or talking. Compared to children his age, he was very slow in walking but with a lot of persistence and patience, one day my efforts were rewarded and Paul started walking all by himself. Unfortunately, this was the beginning of a new nightmare for us.

Little Paul took great delight in running everywhere. He could not believe his new-found freedom but he seemed to be oblivious to the dangers that it posed. The first thing he learnt to do was to unlock and open the front door and rush down the thirteen steps out on to the road. He would dash out without looking sideways and keep on running straight ahead and was hard to catch, and we had many narrow escapes. He would make a run for it when I least expected it and be gone as quick as a flash. We ended up putting slide locks out of his reach on the inside of all our outside doors.

When I had to hang out the washing, he would dash out of the laundry door and tear off into the backyard. He screamed in his usual monotone pitch when he realised that the wooden fence was making him a prisoner and turned circles endlessly with frustration. It was a disturbing thing to witness and I didn't know what to do.

My beautiful new house had become almost like a gaol and I felt like a warder as I followed every step my child took. He suddenly became an expert climber and one day, when I went into the pantry with my back turned for a moment, he had climbed up on to the sink, using the shelf underneath as a step. I came back as I thought I heard water running and saw him actually sitting in the sink, with the hot water tap on, scalding his legs, and laughing. Luckily, I had ice cubes in the freezer and that had saved him from being hospitalised.

Another episode happened in the kitchen, during a hot day when he had no shoes on. He suddenly climbed up to my highest cupboard where I kept my best crystal wine glasses that were a wedding present from my Auntie Louise. He smiled and smashed them all on the floor one by one before I could stop him. Then he jumped down and landed heavily on some of the pieces in his bare feet and then started stuffing bits of glass into his mouth. It was well worth me getting bitten when I was retrieving them as they would have definitely been swallowed and we were so fortunate that his feet had escaped being badly cut. Paul's bizarre behaviour continued but Stan was hardly ever home during daylight hours. Every night I gave Paul his sleeping draught and so when Stan arrived home, all was quiet. He didn't see what I had to contend with every day but at least we got some sleep.

One night, Stan said that his mother, Mildred, wanted to come and see us as she had only seen Paul once before and so Stan had arranged to bring her down for lunch the next day.

I would have appreciated more notice but in the morning, I strapped Paul in his pusher and managed to get some meat pies from the milk bar. I was ready to heat them up when she and Stan arrived. Mildred, of course, had had a lot of experience with her own children but now was a semi-invalid and frail old lady who was quick to dish out advice over lunch.

Paul now had a low chair after an accident rocking and tipping himself over in his high chair. He had landed on the floor with the high chair on top of him and had lost consciousness. Of course, I was terrified and gave him mouth-to-mouth resuscitation until he regained consciousness and Stewart had been wonderful making a house call to check him for concussion. So I was careful to secure Paul in his low chair while we had lunch but I could see that Mildred did not approve of Paul's eating habits. Most of the food that Paul did not want, he squashed with his fingers and spread over the top of his tray table and the rest, he flung all over the walls, furniture and floor. It was amazing to see how and where a Vegemite sandwich could end up.

Mildred, of course, was so critical and said, 'Paul should not be allowed to do such things. As far as I am concerned, he is an attention seeker and very spoilt. What he needs is to be with other children and learn how to behave.' Of course, Stan sided with her but said, 'Lynne is from a small family, Mother, so does not have much experience in bringing up children.'

I found it difficult to argue with them. In my heart I knew that I was doing my very best for my son, even if they did not think so. Then Mildred said, 'Paul should be allowed out of his chair while we finish our meal in peace.'

I firmly disagreed, saying that he needed to be restrained whilst we ate. Of course, I was howled down and when I went to shut the door of the dining room, I was made to feel foolish so I gave in and left it open. Stan did not realise what could happen and so I could not relax as Paul had disappeared down the passage and seemed very quiet. Stan and Mildred were talking all about Stan's wonderful work achievements and as I had heard it all before, I said that I needed to be excused to check on Paul. By then, they had finished their lunch and so followed me.

I heard Mildred say to Stan, 'Lynne is over protective and what Paul really needs is a little brother or sister.' She knew that I had heard her comment, and then she said in a loud, almost commanding voice, 'Practice makes perfect, you know!' And Stan nodded his head in agreement.

As we went into the hall, we all saw the same sight together. Paul had pulled his training pants off and urinated and defecated on the floor. Then he had painted and smeared the mixture all over my beautiful wallpaper right down the passage and over himself, as well. It was a terrible mess and the smell did not go over well after just eating meat pies! Stan and his mother were appalled and made for the front door, as fast as they could, leaving me with all the mess and out of my mind with depression and desperation.

I thought very carefully after Mildred's comments about having another child as I knew that Stan would probably be delighted. Perhaps it was just what Paul needed. I knew that Mum had always said years ago that it was a mistake for couples to only have one child but I wondered how on Earth I would cope with a baby as well as a toddler who could not be tamed or trained.

Yikes! Maybe Mildred was right. Could that be the answer as no one else could help us?

CHAPTER 9

Decisions! Decisions!

After much thought, I decided to try putting Paul in a child-minding centre, so that he could be with other children and also to give me a break to get my house, and myself, in order. Having time just for me was absolute bliss and I could go to the hairdresser by myself. But unfortunately, every child-minding centre refused to have Paul back after the first day, and I couldn't really blame them. The last centre that I tried was in Seaford and when I opened the door, I saw all the children sitting down on the carpet watching *Play School*. We didn't have a TV at home, so it was not surprising when Paul walked right up to it, blocking everyone else's view. However, he was not interested in the show at all and to everyone's surprise, he grabbed hold of the flowers in the vase, on top of the television set, threw them all around the room, and then proceeded to pick up the vase and drink the vile, smelly water.

The lady in charge, Eunice, had never seen anything like it before, and all the children thought it was very funny. I was so upset and apologised profusely. I knew that we were probably going to be shown the door and I couldn't help bursting into tears. I had made an appointment to see Stewart and I did not want to take Paul to the surgery with me. The last time we had been there in the waiting room, he had torn up all the magazines on the coffee table in approximately three minutes flat. I was just about at breaking point when Eunice smiled and said that she would help out, just this once. She had a disused tennis court in the backyard, which the children played in including a cubby house. It was fully fenced of course and she had a lock for the gate. We took Paul down there and he had a wonderful time running from one end to the other, screaming and laughing at the same time. Eunice was sympathetic and said that she was actually a trained nurse and would take care of him until I got back from my appointment. She mentioned that Paul must be a handful at home and that in her opinion he was super hyperactive, which of course, I already knew.

Stewart listened intensely as I told him all about the lunch with my mother-in-law and Stan. I could see that he was very concerned at how I had been treated but then found it hard not to laugh when I told him about Paul and the vase of flowers at the child-minding centre. He could see that things were certainly not getting any better and gave me a referral to see a child psychologist. He said that it would be interesting to get his opinion. When I was leaving, he said, 'Lynne, I know you are going through a very hard time at the moment but just remember that I am always here for you. Now, where's that sweet smile of yours?'

I came home feeling that not all the world was against me.

Stewart had been lovely and Eunice had turned out to be a gem and had offered to have Paul for a few hours in emergencies. I was so grateful and really needed both of their support as I had felt so alone beforehand and did not want to bother my dear mother or sister, with all my worries.

Stan was apprehensive about the referral to the child psychologist but he gave permission for me to arrange a time. Unfortunately, the doctor was running late and we were put into a waiting room with other people waiting for different doctors. It wasn't long before Paul broke away from me and started ripping up magazines and next, he spotted the sheer window curtains like we once had had at home. Everyone stared in disbelief as I caught him and held him on my lap without a cross word or smacking him. However, after about five minutes, things had settled down but then Paul broke free again. This time he was so quick that no one could stop him and none of the ladies were prepared for what happened next. Paul went around to all their handbags left on the floor and up-ended them, in search of lollies. There were cries of embarrassment and panic as the contents of at least five bags were spread all over the floor for everyone to see. There were keys, coins, lipsticks, tissues, personal sanitary products and other items scattered amongst the jumble. The receptionist quickly ushered us into a quiet spare room away from the hullabaloo and the angry mothers who had started to behave like a lynch mob towards me.

However, at long last we got to see Dr Ian Lamont who conducted a series of IQ tests on Paul. Most of the tests proved useless as Paul was not interested in participating, but then all of a sudden, without any instruction, he went over to a wooden jigsaw puzzle and fitted all the pieces into the square. The puzzle was quite advanced and not really meant for a two-and-a-half-year-old. The doctor was impressed but perplexed and said, 'Paul is not unintelligent but is selective in what he wants to do. The closest thing that I can think of that is remotely like Paul's condition is childhood schizophrenia but I am not prepared to diagnose such a drastic outcome as the only things I can be sure of is that Paul is hyperactive and has an intelligence that cannot be accurately measured. I am mystified but Paul may grow out of all these symptoms as he gets older.'

That did it for me! I had no faith in Dr Lamont at all. It had been a waste of time seeing him, particularly as later on reading about childhood schizophrenia in books from the library, I was definitely sure that Paul did not have it.

In the back of my mind, I was still wondering whether another addition to the family would be the answer as I felt that I was back to square one once again.

I decided that maybe it was worth a try, even though we had little sex anymore. I thought that it was now or never. So I decided to be brave and take the chance.

Sue was now studying Junior Secondary Teaching at Mercer House as she had deferred from Monash University after a very successful first year. She had been the youngest female student to start there at the age of seventeen and had worn herself out. I did not see that much of her as she was now busy going on teaching rounds at private boarding schools.

Mum, on the other hand, was doing extremely well with her fashion boutique that she had just bought. I looked forward to her bringing clothes down for me to try on and purchase at cost. She was having the time of her life and loved all aspects of the business, including the buying part, and knew Flinders Lane backwards after being a junior milliner there many years ago.

Suddenly, I felt left out. I was the only one who wasn't progressing and at twenty-five, life seemed to be passing me by. I was getting nowhere. My life was becoming more difficult and even shopping had become impossible.

We had a little supermarket down the road, run by a Greek couple. I had made friends with them when they arrived from Greece and first opened their shop. I used to take Paul shopping there, strapped in his pusher. One day as I was deciding what kind of soup to buy, Paul wriggled out of his harness in the pusher and went up to the display of Heinz soups. It was a symmetrical pyramid of cans and must have taken a long time to assemble. Paul, in his usual fashion, was quick to discover what would happen if he removed some of the bottom cans and in a split second, he had cans tumbling down and rolling all over the floor. There were screams as people's feet and legs were hit by falling tins of soup and other people tripping over them. The whole shop was in chaos.

I was so embarrassed but the nice little Greek couple said not to worry.

However, the next time we went back, I decided to put Paul in a trolley as the store had recently invested in some. He was in his element riding high but soon got very bored when I stopped to select a product or two. Unfortunately, that soon turned out to be a golden opportunity for him to throw everything out of the trolley that I had put in. Customers were hit in the face with all sorts of flying objects but the worst problems of all were the smashed glass bottles of shampoo, tomato sauce and mayonnaise. Customers ducking to miss being hit did not notice what was on the floor and slipped and slid over the sticky mess with bits of glass attaching to the soles of their shoes and clothes. Paul had caused a disaster. I knew that I could never go in there again with him, so I wasn't surprised when the nice little Greek couple suggested that I phone them with my order in future and they would deliver it to my door. We had been banned, for life!

One afternoon, I decided to take Paul to the beach. I had been feeling a bit queasy in the mornings and missed my period, so I had a feeling that I was pregnant again and I needed some fresh air. As Paul was now three years old, I thought that he might like to walk on the Frankston Pier as I had done at his age on the way to Rosebud for our Christmas holidays.

It was such a joy to feel the sand as I slipped off my thongs when we hit the beach. Paul had his harness on with reins attached and seemed to love the sand as much as I did; only he began eating handfuls of it. Thankfully he stopped when we made it to the pier and Paul loved walking on it but when we were nearly at the end, when he wanted to keep on going. He wanted to walk off the end and into the sea! It was an unnerving experience! He had no fear at all. It was as if he thought he could walk on water. I found great difficulty in trying to stop him from pulling us both over and into the waves below as there was no safety railing at that spot. Luckily there was a man fishing nearby, who saved us, just as I was beginning to lose control. I couldn't believe the strength that Paul had had and was so grateful to him. I thanked him a million times as he escorted us off the pier and back into the car. He said that Paul was a lovely looking kid but that he would not like to have my job, looking after him full time. He couldn't get over Paul's strength either. I offered him a reward but he would not take any money for helping me.

When we got home, I began to realise that nothing would ever be the same for me again. Even going to the beach would not be possible. I began to feel miserable and decided to ring the surgery and make an appointment to see Stewart. Then I rang Eunice and she was very kind and agreed to mind Paul for me and from then on, I managed to pay her extra.

At the appointment, I gave Stewart an update on all that had been happening, including the shopping disasters and the supermarket ban. He was amazed at the Frankston Pier episode and even more when I said that I thought I could be pregnant.

He examined me and said, 'You are right, Lynne. The baby is due in the middle of July.' Then he became serious and said, 'Do you really want to have another child?'

'Yes,' I said. 'I certainly do, because I believe that it is worth a try to help Paul become a normal child and I would do anything for that to happen!'

Stewart looked at me, the same way that Joel had looked at me at the Orbost Comfort Station when he asked me, 'What did you do that for?' when I told him I had just got married to Stan.

All at once, I felt that maybe I had made another fatal mistake and I wondered what was wrong with me.

Stewart must have seen the look of panic on my face and immediately reassured me.

'I now understand perfectly how you feel. You are a wonderful mother. When you come for your next check-up, I will give you a referral to see the top gynaecologist/obstetrician in Melbourne. So there is no need to be worried. This time you will be under the best of care.'

Suddenly I felt so much better as I knew that I was doing the right thing after all.

Stewart smiled and gave me the thumbs up as I left his room, filled with regained confidence.

Chapter 10

New Happenings

Stan was over the moon with pride and joy when I told him the news and couldn't wait to tell his mother. I explained that now I was home for most of the time and not feeling that well, I needed a TV set. I offered to pay it off, on hire purchase, out of my housekeeping money but Stan was very nice and said that he would take care of it. I was so happy when it arrived and it helped to keep me in touch with the outside world as Paul and I had been virtually cut off from going anywhere.

My gynaecologist was an Irishman, Dr Brian O'Leary, and his rooms were in Collins Street in the city. He was a lovely man and full of fun.

On my first appointment, I had a nervous walk up Collins Street to the renowned medical section. My mind was full, having Paul with an unknown locum, so now I knew I was in very safe and professional hands with Brian and I felt so relieved.

I enjoyed every visit and he completely put me at ease about every aspect of my pregnancy and the birth. He had a large family himself and said that no two single pregnancies were ever alike. I suspected Stewart had written to him regarding my fears and so I was grateful that I was in such good hands. I was booked into St Vincent's Private Maternity Hospital and although I wasn't a Catholic, Dr O'Leary said that it didn't matter as the Catholic Sisters would be very happy to look after me.

After the first three to four months, my morning sickness disappeared and although I was really very tired all the time, I could not complain. Now that we had a smart eighteen-inch TV set on legs, I didn't mind being shut inside so much with Paul. A new serial called *Days of Our Lives* had just started and I loved it. All the actresses were so glamorous and the male actors were very good-looking. The storylines were ridiculous but really helped to get my mind off my own problems as there always seemed to be unbelievable and intriguing situations in every episode. It was my escape! I did not venture out much at all as Paul was getting stronger every day. I could not manage him even with the reins on and I was frightened that he might pull me over and I could hurt or lose the baby.

During this time, I did miss having someone to talk to but Mum was too busy and Sue was away teaching at an exclusive boarding school, Clyde, for young ladies at Mount Macedon, and I didn't like to bother them or Stewart as I was Dr O'Leary's patient. I became almost like a recluse and lived my life watching over Paul and preventing him from injuring himself or running away. Day and night blended into one another and seemed to have no ending. With no one having any idea what was wrong with Paul, I just had to hope and pray that having a little brother or sister might make all the difference or that he would grow out of this strange behaviour. Maybe someone would find out what was wrong with him. I got tired of turning all these thoughts over in my mind, day after day. It was hopeless trying to communicate with Stan as he was too focused on his ambition to be a millionaire and always quoted his mother's convictions.

On 16th July 1968, our second son, Hayden, was born. He was the dearest little thing and so placid. I could hardly believe that he was real. When I first held him, he looked straight into my eyes. I loved him so much and Dr O'Leary assured me that he was physically perfect and I thanked God.

Mum had been minding Paul when I was in hospital and when she came to see me without him, I was terrified that she had left him alone with Dad. She said that there was no need to worry as it was the weekend and Sue had come all the way home from the mountain to help look after him. I was so grateful to my sister but in the back of my mind, I wondered if our dear mother had any idea what Dad had been up to the day of Paul's first birthday party.

At the end of the week, Stan drove us home and baby Hayden and I settled in very well. The darling little sweetheart was so good and only cried when hungry or wet. The next day, Mum and Sue brought Paul home and all chaos broke loose. Mum had been absolutely wonderful minding Paul but was utterly exhausted. I was so grateful that Sue had driven them down as I could see Mum was worn out. She admitted that she could not have managed at all, without the sleeping medication prescribed for Paul, even though it only seemed to work for about six hours a night.

The long-anticipated moment arrived when we showed Hayden to Paul. How disappointed we were when he did not even glance at him. He was not a scrap interested in his new brother, or anyone, for that matter. There was still no eye contact with me and when I tried to cuddle him, he pushed me away as usual. I was deeply hurt but it was typical of him. It was as if he was the only one in the world and nobody else meant anything to him. I had missed him when I was in the hospital but at the same time, it was a huge relief not having to be on duty day and night and listen to Paul's monotone moaning all the time. I felt guilty having these feelings but it was the truth.

Sue and Mum adored the new baby but were worried how I was going to manage. It had been bad enough before and the house had always been in a dreadful mess. I had to lock all the cleaning aids in the garage otherwise Paul would have drunk or eaten them. Everything still went in his mouth even though he was now three years and eight months. Mum said that she would love to help me but she had already spent a week away from her business and in any case, lived too far away. Then she suggested that I ask Stan if I could have a lady come in one morning a week and give the house a thorough clean. It would not cost the Earth and would help me deal with one of my biggest problems. I thought it was a brilliant idea and was determined to get some help as dear little Hayden deserved my love and attention just as much as Paul did.

After Mum and Sue went, I warmed up a bottle for the baby and we went into the TV room, which was a spare bedroom with a single bed and was stripped of things that Paul could destroy. I had found my nursery chair in an opportunity shop and repainted it early in my pregnancy. It was so comfortable as it had arms in the right place and Mum had made me a new cushion.

I sat down in front of the television and started to feed Hayden whilst watching the news. He was so good. I had locked us all in the room to prevent Paul from running out without supervision but this really angered him, more than usual. Perhaps he wasn't used to our old routine again after spending time away from home. I did not know, but he exploded into a violent temper tantrum, screaming and flapping his arms up and down. He was behaving like a caged animal. Then there was a crash and in a fit of rage, my beautiful new TV set had been pushed over on the floor. I suddenly realised that things with Paul were not going to be any better and I cried, hopelessly!

After seeing the smashed TV set, Stan agreed to me having some domestic help. I advertised in the local paper and had about twenty replies. The ladies were so nice and really wanted to help me. As I could not engage everyone, I promised them all I would find jobs for them working elsewhere. My new business was born and I called it Sadie's Ladies. I advertised that I had ladies available to do housework in private homes and was inundated with calls. It was very successful and the beauty of it was that it could be run from home.

The lady I chose for myself was Amanda who was a young mothercraft nurse and worked at the Frankston Hospital in midwifery and was saving up for a trip overseas. She was lovely and we got on so well. She was like a breath of fresh air and came every Monday morning. This meant that I could actually leave Hayden with her and take Paul to Eunice to be minded and be free to go to the dentist, hairdresser or attend to whatever I needed to do. It was like being let out of gaol for three hours each week.

I did not know how I managed to carry on my little business at home with an out-of-control child and a baby, but I knew if I was to survive, I had to keep my sanity. Talking on the phone with people, listening to their requirements and then matching them with my team of ladies gave me the opportunity to keep in touch with the real world. Surprisingly enough, Stan was all for it and bragged to his friends that I had started a cleaning business.

During my pregnancy, I had over-eaten comfort food and was

overweight compared to what I had been so I decided to go on a diet. It was easy once I put my mind to it. Stan did not eat at home much anymore, with the exception of breakfast. So, with no other meals to cook, I found it simple to restrict what I ate. I was delighted when after three months I could fit back into my old clothes comfortably. The next thing I decided to do was to change my hair. The hairdresser suggested blonde streaks but after she had finished, it neither looked like one colour or another and I hated it. The following week, I decided to go blonde all over and I was really pleased with the result. Everyone, including Stan, liked it and it gave me a tremendous lift. I had to keep thinking of things that would make me happy, as underneath, I knew that I was in danger of becoming very depressed as Paul was getting worse. Little Hayden made eye contact with me and showed affection. He was far more advanced than Paul was at his age. Deep in my heart, I knew that there was really something abnormal about Paul but sadly I had run out of options to pursue.

Then, one day, I read an article in the latest *Women's Weekly* magazine about a new childhood condition that had just been diagnosed. It was called *autism*. There were fourteen symptoms listed and Paul had thirteen of them. I was shell-shocked! I read and re-read them over and over again. It was almost as if someone had written a list of every single thing that was abnormal and bizarre about Paul's behaviour. The symptoms that Paul had were thirteen out of fourteen, as follows:

1. No eye contact.
2. Lack of speech.
3. Flat facial expression and vocal tone.
4. No interest in other children.
5. Selective hearing.
6. Dislike of being cuddled or picked up.
7. Inability to cope with change.
8. Impaired lack of understanding of environment.
9. Inexplicable tantrums.
10. Over or under sensitivity to sound, taste, smell, touch or light.
11. Unusual attachments to objects and textures.
12. Unimaginative and repetitive play.

13. Unusual persistent body movements, such as flapping of the arms and walking on tiptoes.

A tremendous fear came over me as I realised that my first-born child could be autistic.

I showed the article to Stan when he came home and he scoffed at it and said that I was overreacting. He said that he was tired and didn't want to read anything at 11.30 pm. He just wanted to get to bed and sleep. However, I said that I was going to see Dr Applegate the next day and see what he had to say about it.

It was always comforting for me to see Stewart. He was so supportive and eager to help and this day was no exception. I came straight to the point and showed him the magazine article with all the symptoms that applied to Paul ticked off. He studied it carefully and then looked at me, straight in the eyes and said very seriously, 'Lynne, I think you may be right. I have never heard of autism before. May I borrow this, so that I can read it through thoroughly tonight? I'll give it back to you tomorrow. Make an appointment to see me in the afternoon as I will be making a few telephone calls in the morning about this condition.'

I started to feel very frightened as the last sentence of the article had said that there was no cure for the condition. Tears sprouted automatically and I seemed to be so alone. As I stood up to leave, I suddenly felt Stewart's arms around me as he gave me a hug. It felt wonderful and before I knew it, I had hugged him back and we had parted with a gentle kiss on the lips.

I went home with mixed emotions. I was so worried about Paul. Part of me was dreading tomorrow but of course, the other part of me could not wait to see Stewart again. How could this be? I felt as if I was falling in love! After reliving the whole consultation in my mind, again and again, I suddenly realised that I was a married woman and that as far as I knew, he was also married. I knew that I had been starved of real love and affection for a long time, and so maybe I had misinterpreted the whole thing. Perhaps Stewart had just felt sorry for me. I didn't know. The only thing I did know was that I kept thinking about him. I had felt so secure in his arms and I longed to feel that way again.

Stan was home even later that evening and when I told him that I would know more tomorrow about Paul's condition, he was furious. 'What kind of a doctor is Applegate if he has to read a women's rag to find out what is wrong with his patients? Anyway, I think you are both barking up the wrong tree.'

I fell asleep not worrying about what Stan thought. In fact, I couldn't care less about him.

Chapter 11

A Glimmer of Hope

The next day, Eunice was very understanding and had consented to look after Paul again. I was so lucky to have her and her tennis court. She was just as anxious to find out what was actually wrong with him as I was. It was Amanda's housework day and she was happy to look after Hayden for me. I was in a very mixed-up state of mind and needed to sort everything out that was going on in my head without taking him with me to my appointment.

Stewart gave me some very flattering compliments about my clothes and hair. Then he said, 'I have never met a braver young lady than you ever before.' I had a feeling that all of this was to break the ice before he told me the bad news and I was right.

He said, 'I contacted the Mental Health Authority and spoke to Dr Shane Patterson, a new child psychiatrist at the Travancore Clinic, who has just started specialising in autism. His initial feeling was that it was more than likely that Paul was autistic but of course, he would have to see him. So I have made an appointment for you and Paul to see Dr Patterson next week.' I was prepared for the worst but also, I was determined to do the best for my child and would stop at nothing to find out at last what was wrong with him and how I could cure him. Then Stewart asked, 'How is Stan taking all of this?'

I had to be truthful and caved in. 'It's as if he just doesn't want to know. He is in denial.'

'Oh! You don't have to face this on your own, you know, Lynne,' said Stewart. 'Don't forget, I will always be here for you. I really do care what happens, you know.'

I was so grateful that at last I could count on someone who understood me and how I felt.

I melted into his arms and this time I knew it was true; I had fallen desperately in love with him and he seemed to feel the same way about me. This time our kisses were real ones and stayed with me until I saw him again. I couldn't believe it! What a strange time to be falling in love again! I was at my lowest ebb and the only thing that kept me going was thinking about Stewart and the kisses we had shared.

I felt very guilty about having these feelings. I had been brought up to believe that what I was thinking was a sin. Adultery was one of the Ten Commandments and absolutely forbidden. Yet I still found myself craving for Stewart, in every possible way. How could I allow myself to be so weak and how could I have thoughts of being unfaithful to my husband? It went against all my standards but it seemed to have engulfed me and what is more, I really did not want to fight it.

Perhaps, I was really a bad person and Paul's illness was my punishment. It was hard for me to understand what was happening and I was too ashamed to tell anyone how I felt. Mum would have had a fit! The other thing that worried me was that when I was with Stewart, I felt happy and safe. How could I feel like that when I should have been completely engrossed in Paul?

My poor little boy was not really happy or safe. I should not have been contemplating anything that would bring me happiness when Paul needed me so much. But try as I may, I could not get Stewart out of my mind.

At the Travancore Clinic, Dr Patterson was delightful and very professional. It did not take him long to diagnose Paul as being *Profoundly Autistic*. He tried to break it to me gently and even though I was prepared for the worst, I found it impossible not to burst into tears. Dr Patterson offered me a box of tissues and as I made use of some them, Paul grabbed the box and took great delight in ripping the rest of the tissues into shreds and showering them all over the room. Then he broke free from my grip and went around the doctor's desk, picked up a ball point pen, pulled out the refill and starting chewing it up. After I had rescued him from that, he proceeded to wrench the extension phone out of its socket and smash it to pieces on the tiled floor. Dr Patterson took it all in his stride as if he was used to such things. He gave me a prescription for a new drug called Valium to help calm Paul down. Then he gave me details of a small self-help group of parents who had autistic children, which went under the name of the Victorian Autistic Children's Association. Apparently, they had started a school for their children, which was still in the experimental stage. Then he said that he would like to see me in a fortnight's time to check on us both as he was concerned about my health also. He was such a nice man.

That night, Stan flew into a rage when I told him of Dr Patterson's findings. He said that as there was nothing in his family's history anything like autism and it was quite clear that it must be on my side of the family and, in fact, my entire fault!

Completely crushed by his cruel accusations, I defended my family vehemently but it went on deaf ears and I went to bed without speaking to him. Secretly, I felt totally rejected and wished that Stewart could have been there to comfort me.

The next day, I telephoned Jan Barnett who was a mother from the Victorian Autistic Children's Association and happened to live near me in Mount Eliza. She had an eight-year-old son who was attending the experimental school and offered to drive me there when she went to collect him that afternoon. She sounded so friendly and we spent a long time talking about our children's similarities.

It was so good to speak to someone who was experiencing what I was going through. Jan promised to pick me up at the Seaford Child Minding Centre on the way through to the school, which was in a church hall in Cheltenham.

Eunice very kindly took Paul and Hayden for me, without much prior notice, as she had a lovely young assistant Belinda, who was in charge of caring for the babies. Eunice was all ears when I told her of the diagnosis from the day before and was very sympathetic but also relieved that at last we knew what was wrong with Paul.

Jan arrived on time and we had another long talk in her car all the way to the school. She said, 'I am so pleased that this school is helping my little boy, Nicky, but unfortunately they may not have any places left for any more children.'

There were two young female teachers at the hall and I could see by the way they treated the children that they were dedicated. I noticed that even though the children were all autistic, they were not all the same. Some had lesser problems than others but they all had problems one way or another. One little boy was a climber and his father had had to get special permission from the church to put rows of barbed wire on the top of the cyclone fence to stop his son from climbing over it and running away. There were nine children there and, in my opinion, they needed more than two teachers but of course, money was a real issue as the parents had to pay for everything. When all the other children were picked up by their parents, Jan introduced me to the teachers.

Donna and Sandra were lovely and listened intently as I described Paul. At four and a half, he was the youngest one they had heard of to be diagnosed. They explained that as autism was a new discovery, there was no guarantee that it could be cured but at least some symptoms could be addressed. I was very eager for Paul to start at the school as soon as possible but was dismayed when told that there was not enough room for even one more child. In fact, the hall was not going to be available for them either as the church had sold the block of land it was on and it was going to be demolished very soon so they were flat out finding new premises for the existing pupils.

I suddenly had an idea and asked them if I found a place for them, larger than the hall they had, would they consider taking Paul. They were taken aback and looked at me as if I was mad. I think they thought that they were dealing with a 'pie in the sky' notion. Then I asked them if they minded if I got a television station involved. Their faces lit up and after consideration, Donna said, 'We think it is a brilliant idea and will get the parents' permission for you to go ahead.' I went home feeling happy as I had just taken an important step in fighting for my child's future.

When the teachers had the all clear from the parents, I phoned the ABC and they were very interested to hear about the saddest school in Melbourne being forced to close down, through no fault of its own. Suddenly it all happened. A film crew came out to the hall the next day and Peter Couchman interviewed me on *This Day Tonight*. They wanted to shoot footage of me sitting on a swing with Paul but he would not sit still long enough. So I was interviewed alone, stating the case on behalf of all the children, parents and teachers. The producer of the show named it 'The Saddest School in Melbourne'.

I got an encouraging phone call from Mum, who had been devastated to hear the news about Paul not being accepted at the school. However, she said that she would be very surprised if the association did not get new premises for it after seeing my heart-wrenching plea on TV and even Auntie Louise, an ex-army nurse, had seen it in New South Wales and sent her love. Mum apologised for not being able to assist in my efforts but she was doing so well in her business that she had just opened another boutique. Of course, I understood and I was so pleased for her. I had plans also of opening an office for my little housework service and employing someone to run it as I never had enough hours in the day to cope with the demand. We were both becoming entrepreneurs and enjoyed the cash flow that went with it.

Next day, Sandra, one of the teachers, rang me and she was overjoyed. The TV show had produced a great response and the parents had decided to take up an offer of a church hall in Mentone. It was in the vicinity of the other one and therefore, would suit all the parents. Then she said that they would be moving in the following week and when they were settled, Paul could start. I was so thrilled and thanked her from the bottom of my heart.

I couldn't wait to tell Stewart all the news and was lucky to get an appointment with him due to a late cancellation that afternoon. I phoned Eunice and she said that she would not mind caring for Paul and Hayden. I was so lucky having her on my side.

Stewart had had a full report on Paul sent to him from Dr Patterson and he was pleased that I had related so well with him. Then Stewart started complimenting me on my compelling interview on *This Day Tonight*, which he just happened to be watching.

I had great pleasure in telling him the wonderful result and he said, 'I'm not surprised. I knew you could do it, Lynne! I'm so proud of you.'

Then he held me close and I started to get that old familiar feeling that I had not had for years.

We looked into each other's eyes with passionate desire and he kissed me as I had never been kissed before.

Then he whispered in my ear, 'When Paul is settled, would you like me to pay you a special home visit?'

Chapter 12

Unforgettable Moments

Stan's reaction to my moment of fame and glory on TV was non-existent as he wasn't home to see it. He regarded everything I had done for Paul in the past week or so as a waste of time. He had no faith in Dr Patterson or the autistic school. However, he did make a surprising comment. 'Seeing you are the one who had Paul, then you should be the one to look after him and I will not interfere.' I was really upset and hurt by his attitude. I felt as if he had washed his hands of supporting me in my endeavours to secure our son's future. The only thing he seemed really interested in was my home help agency, Sadie's Ladies.

It wasn't long before Stan had found an office for me in Mount Eliza. Neil Rayner, who was an accountant and a partner of Terra Firma, had some spare space at the back of his offices, upstairs in the village. He was very kind and said that I could sublease it from him for a peppercorn rental of forty-five dollars a month until I got established. I advertised for a manager and it wasn't very long before I found Mrs Cooper, who had worked in a government employment office. She was a great help and taught me their card systems, et cetera. It was bliss not having to run my business from home anymore and it continued to thrive.

My next visit to Dr Patterson at Travancore was less traumatic. He was pleased that I had contacted Jan and he had actually seen me on *This Day Tonight*. He was extremely impressed when I told him that the school was moving to Mentone as a result of my efforts, and that Paul would be starting there the following week. I told him that because of the Valium, Paul had calmed down quite considerably but had refused to take the crushed tablet in honey after a while as he was clever enough to realise that it slowed him down. I said that I felt really bad about having to drug my child as particularly, I ended up putting the Valium in his ice cream, which was his favourite food and he ate it without knowing.

Then the doctor started asking questions about my relationship with Stan and I confessed. 'I am not getting any support from him and I think that we are drifting apart.'

Dr Patterson replied, 'I am afraid that in these cases, it is not uncommon for the husband to do "the ostrich act" and that couples are either brought very much closer together, or the exact opposite occurs. However, I would like to see Paul again in a fortnight's time, to see how he is adapting to the new school. A good result, hopefully, may help with your husband's reasoning.'

Soon, it was Paul's first day at the school and I drove Paul and Nicky to Mentone while Hayden was being minded by Amanda. After handing over spare clothes and training pants for Paul, I left him in Donna and Sandra's care but upon our return in the afternoon, the teachers had disturbing news for me. They had never seen such a bad case of autism ever before and Paul had disrupted the whole school from the moment I had left. Both teachers were very kind and tried to be understanding but the welfare of the other children had to be considered also. They said that it had taken the two of them just to look after Paul and they were concerned that unless he settled down, they would have no alternative but to ask me to withdraw him from the school. However, they said that they were willing to have him on a trial basis until the end of the week. I was shattered! It took me all my strength to drop Nicky off to Jan on the way home.

That night, I told Stan what had happened at the school but he was totally unaffected.

'They are a group of do-gooders that do not have a clue what they were doing. I could have told you that and saved you wasting your time with them. By the way, how is Mrs Cooper going at your office?'

'I am happy to report that she is going very well and the business is increasing rapidly after my recent idea of expanding the local business to going all over Melbourne. She agreed it was time and added useful tips to my advice on how we should proceed. So now I am thinking of trading in Mum's old Morris Minor for an as-new, second-hand white Karmann Ghia sports car. I have seen one in a Frankston car yard and have enough money for a deposit. What do you think?'

Stan was thrilled and nodded. 'I can't wait to tell Neil and the others. Well done!'

The next day it was my turn to drive the boys to the school and I did it without any trouble. Hayden sat in his car seat in the front and the two boys in the back. They both liked riding in the back seat of the Morris Minor and seemed quite happy to retreat into their own worlds and did not seem to be aware that the other one was sitting next to them. It was very strange to watch them in the rear-vision mirror. When I arrived, I could see the teachers were eager to make a superhuman effort with Paul and I loved them for it.

On the way home, I dropped Hayden off at the child-minding centre and found Eunice in tears. She had just received a final notice from the council advising her that she had to move her business elsewhere in seven days as they had had objections from the neighbours regarding noise and parking. Her old permit had expired and they were not giving her a chance to renew it at that address. She told me that she thought she may have an opportunity of renting a friend's house on the Nepean Highway but unfortunately for me, it had no tennis court. So of course that meant that I would have nowhere to leave Paul if he was not allowed to continue at Mentone. We both had a little cry together and I tried to support her as she had done for me in the past.

I had made an appointment to see Stewart later that morning. He was busy but had told his staff always to squeeze me in if I phoned. As I went into his room, he could see that I was very upset and he immediately put his arms around me. We sat down and I explained what had happened at the school. Tears came into my eyes as I feared the worst. I knew Paul would not get any better and that after the end of this week, I would be back to square one but it would be even worse now without Eunice's help. It was so disappointing. I had gone through all the trouble of getting new premises for a school that maybe was going to ban my son! It didn't seem fair and all of a sudden, I felt exhausted!

Stewart got up and came around his desk and stood opposite me. Then he reached out for my hands. He kissed the pads of each of my fingers and thumbs and then the back of my fingers, closing each of my hands with one of his. Then he held both our hands up together, against his heart and kissed my forehead. It was beautiful. His English accent suddenly sounded very soft and seductive as he asked me if tomorrow at two o'clock would suit me for a house call. My heart pounded as I nodded my head slowly and we both knew what he meant.

All the way in the car driving up to the school, I kept thinking of what had just transpired and wondered if this was really happening to me. I knew very well why Stewart was coming to see me tomorrow and I wanted him as much as he wanted me. If only we both weren't married! I knew it wasn't right and I knew that it would not be too late to put it off but then I realised that I was in too deep to back out now. I was past caring what anyone thought. I was in a trance. My head was filled with excited anticipation and my heart was filled with the deepest of love.

I was elated and was not going to let anyone or anything spoil it.

Surprisingly, Donna and Sandra had good news for me when I picked up the boys. Paul had had a slightly better day but they still had great concerns. However, as there were three more days to go before the end of the week, they were reserving their final judgment until Friday. I brightened up and tried to be positive again. Maybe a miracle would happen. Paul would improve. I was quite surprised at my change in attitude and for once, I did not feel that I was entirely alone. I knew why, of course. I had Stewart on my side and felt so lucky.

The next day, Jan arrived to pick up Paul as it was her turn to drive the boys to school and back. I had counted on her being available as we had planned or otherwise, my meeting with Stewart could not have been considered.

Jan was very supportive and said that she hoped Paul would be able to continue at Mentone. She was keen for both the boys to get better and also because it helped her to have someone to share the driving. She was so sweet and said that she should be back at four o'clock with the teachers' daily progress report.

After dropping Hayden off with Eunice, I was in such an excited mood that I decided to buy my new dream car. I was sad to say goodbye to the old Morris Minor but on arriving home, cleaning the house and changing the sheets on the bed did not seem like a chore. I had discovered my best pink percale sheet set, which had been a wedding present, at the back of the linen cupboard. They had never been used before and I knew they would be perfect. Then I showered and washed my hair and ate a light lunch. Suddenly, I started to feel jittery and wondered what I should wear. This was all new to me! I didn't know whether to wear a dress or one of my nighties and negligee that I never wore any more but I decided to wear a new frock that Mum had sold me. It was a buttoned-through shirtmaker style, in cream linen, with a straight skirt and a wide belt that showed off my narrow waist and looked very smart with my matching patent leather stiletto heel shoes.

When the doorbell rang, I timidly opened the front door. Stewart was standing there in his golf clothes as every Wednesday afternoon he had off, playing golf. I invited him in and immediately nervously asked him if he would like a cup of tea. He smiled as I think he knew I had never done anything like this before and then suddenly he swept me up into his strong arms and carried me off into the bedroom.

He set me down on the bed with its pretty, pink sheets looking invitingly at us. Then all at once we were in each other's arms and kissing like I had remembered we had in the surgery, only this time it was even better. I was so happy and when he started to unbutton my dress, I was thankful that I had bought a new lace bra with matching bikini briefs.

Stewart was a very handsome man and looked and sounded exactly like the film star Roger Moore. I had always loved the TV series of *The Saint* and later the *James Bond* films. It was no wonder that I found Stewart irresistible. I had never felt like this before. My desire for him kept building up. Soon I found out what *real foreplay* was all about. He was very gentle and kept on giving me compliments as he kissed and caressed me. I was in raptures when he kissed every part of my body and to my surprise, I experienced the most intense orgasm when he tenderly massaged my clitoris with his warm, moist tongue. It was so beautiful and so unexpected. I had never known such things were possible as up until that day, I had not even known that I had a clitoris, let alone the power it had. I felt as if I had been propelled to another world and never wanted it to end. He was a very skilful lover, and being a doctor, knew exactly how and where to excite me and make me want more.

Next moment, he told me to get ready for the best time I was about to have in my life and then it happened. It was unbelievable, feeling him inside me. He was rock solid and in no hurry. He encouraged me to let myself go and have as many orgasms as I wanted. Amazingly, he stayed erect, while I had two more. Only after all that did he think of himself and ask me if I was ready for the big one that we would have together. I wasn't sure whether I had the strength for another one but somehow, he knew that I would and our love-making ended simultaneously in one enormous explosion of passion. We were both exhausted and dripping with perspiration and collapsed into each other's arms, resting entwined, underneath one of the pink sheets whilst my head remained in the clouds.

Time had flown and it was soon half past three! Stewart went into the bathroom and had a shower. I found it difficult to get dressed again as I was still in a state of euphoria and had not really come down to Earth yet.

I had just had the most incredible afternoon and discovered things about my body that I had never known. I had had multiple orgasms and my first experience of oral sex. I had read about it but never thought that I would ever experience it. I felt as if I would never be the same again. Stewart looked fresh and said that he'd better get going. I asked him jokingly if he wanted a cup of tea and he said that he would have one next time. I was so pleased he had hinted at a *next time* because I knew now that I could not live without him. I hoped that he was feeling the same way about me and so asked him.

'What do you think of me, Stewart?'

'I think you're wonderful!' he said and blew me a kiss as he waved goodbye.

CHAPTER 13

Ups and Downs

On Friday afternoon I was still walking on air after Wednesday's unforgettable assignation. Unfortunately, my happiness was short-lived as I got the news that I was dreading. Paul was unsuitable for the autistic school. The teachers were very upset at having to tell me that my son could not continue there and Jan and I were equally disappointed. I had run into a brick wall and felt absolutely flattened and wondered what on Earth I was going to do.

Then suddenly, I thought that they might agree to an alternative proposition. As it was Christmas in a few weeks, I asked them if they would consider having Paul for two days a week until they broke up, pleading that I had Hayden and a business to look after and no one to care for Paul. They could see by the look on my face that I was desperate and the fact that I had been the one to get them the new bigger and better hall made them relent. I was so grateful and on the way home, Jan said that she was glad that I had come up with the two days a week idea for Paul's sake and for her sake as well as she was going to miss me.

The next week, I went to see Dr Patterson who had decided to be on first name terms with me from now on. Shane was not surprised at the teachers' dilemma. He explained, 'Paul, after all, is Profoundly Autistic and it is unlikely that anything can be done for him until they find a cure which could be years away, if ever.' He tried to be kind and gave me full marks for trying to find a place for Paul but I could see in his eyes that he thought I was fighting a losing battle. I asked him what caused autism and he said, 'No one knows.' I also asked him if it could be genetic as I was still haunted by Stan's accusations. Shane was quick to reply and said, 'There is no reason to believe that it is hereditary.'

He was sickened when I told him about my husband blaming me and my family for Paul's condition. Shane was very understanding and so I told him that I was fearful as to what would happen to me in the future. I could not see myself being able to care for Paul forever, as I had Hayden to think of and I was so sleep deprived now that I did not know how I could continue on if I had to manage him at home full-time. Shane could see I was nearly at breaking point and had a suggestion.

'After the autistic school breaks up, you should bring Paul into the short-term, residential section of Travancore for a weekend. This would give you a break and Stan and you could go away for a little holiday and try to rescue your marriage.' Even though I really did not want to save my marriage, I did want to save my sanity and so of course, I agreed.

He buzzed the office of the matron and arranged for me to see her there and then, and before I left his room, he wrote out a prescription for me. It was for Valium, the same drug as Paul was having. He said, 'I am worried that you could be on the verge of nervous breakdown and you need to calm down.' I was quite alarmed but then, I did trust him.

I found the matron's office and knocked on the door with anticipation. Matron Edna Wilson was a motherly kind of lady and I liked her immediately. She made Paul's booking for three nights commencing on Friday 17th December so that I could admit him that afternoon and we could get an early start on our break the next day. Then she showed me the accommodation building, which was homely and much better than I had thought it would be.

Stan hit the roof at me for arranging a weekend away from his precious work. Finally, after a lot of persuasion, he decided we could go away and stay for the Saturday night only, so that he could be back early on the Sunday morning as that was the busiest day when most prospective clients visited his display homes. I really did not care if we went away or not as I knew in my heart that it was useless for us to try and save our marriage. I would have been just pleased to have three nights of peaceful sleep no matter where we were. Of course, I knew that Matron Wilson and Shane expected me to try and keep my end of the bargain and so I told Stan that I wanted to go to Rosebud and stay at *Wenona*. After a while, he reluctantly agreed as it was not too far away.

The only part I was really looking forward to was going back to Rosebud again, even staying only one night and showing Hayden the beach and boat shed. I certainly did not want to try and patch up a hopeless marriage that I now realised had been a mistake from the beginning.

I hadn't been back to *Wenona* for ages. It had been my sanctuary, growing up happily during summer holidays from when I was a toddler. My dearest Auntie Beth and Uncle Bill owned a delightful cottage with outside bungalows and leased a boat shed on the foreshore. They were like surrogate parents to me and very kind. It was the highlight of my life and I always felt so safe and loved by the whole family who used to pop in on day trips every Christmas.

Next morning, I had an appointment with Stewart at his new surgery that he and the other partner doctors had built. It looked very smart and modern. The usual receptionists were there and made me feel at ease. They had been hard at work helping with the move and were very relieved when I arrived without Paul as he always left a trail of destruction behind him, which they had to clean up. They were always nice to me though and I knew they pitied me.

As I sat in a chair waiting, my heart started thumping madly when Stewart appeared in his white coat with a stethoscope around his neck and called out my name. His new room was spacious and smelt pristine. Immediately, he shut the door. I was in his arms. We both knew what we wanted to do but of course had to control ourselves and sat down. I had a lot to tell him and he sympathised at my disappointment about the autistic school banning Paul. The next thing was that he did not like the sound of my night away with Stan at Rosebud. I detected a streak of jealousy and concern, so I consoled him with a loving kiss and stressed that this would not affect our relationship as my marriage had no hope of ever being rescued.

Then I suddenly realised something important. 'Next Wednesday afternoon will be my last free afternoon before Paul's school breaks up. Would you like to see me then?'

He immediately cheered up and said, 'I can't wait! But this time I would like you to come to my place as my wife and children will be away on holidays overseas.' So I arranged to meet him in the car park after his morning surgery finished at approximately one o'clock.

Just as I was about to leave, we stood up and he looked at me, longingly, and said, 'I am afraid that this is what you do to me, Lynne!'

To my great amazement, he opened his medical coat to reveal his masculinity, which was fully erect and much larger than I remembered. Before I knew what was happening, he had placed my hand around it and was showing me how give him pleasure. At the same time, he had his other hand up my skirt and was gently reciprocating. I was completely blown away as my mind went back to the oral sex I had had the other day. This was exciting too and absolutely exquisite. I couldn't help it and started to moan. I was terrified that the whole waiting room could hear but Stewart said not to worry as the new rooms were completely soundproof. Then after it was all over, we kissed, and then I floated out the door, realising that no one else outside in the waiting room had a clue what had just happened!

Another thing that made me happy was that Mum was doing so well with her shops and I let her know that there was a new vacant shop in the Mount Eliza Village. On the other hand, I wanted to expand my business all over Melbourne and when I had advertised for a lady to clean Mum's house in Mount Waverley, the response had been overwhelming. I had interviewed over thirty women at one of Mum's shops that had living quarters at the back. I covered the walls of my office in Mount Eliza with street maps of mainly the eastern suburbs and started advertising the service in their local papers. The demand for domestic help just before Christmas was much greater than I had anticipated and I spent as much time as I could in the office helping Mrs Cooper, or Olive, as I now called her. I was so glad that I had a lady like her and I trusted her implicitly. In the back of my mind, I had plans of opening another office closer to the city to cope with all my new clients and interviewing cleaning ladies. I really enjoyed my little business and felt that it was keeping me sane.

It wasn't long before Wednesday arrived and I packed Paul off with Jan and Nicky to Mentone. I would be driving the boys on Friday for the last time, so I was determined to make the most of my afternoon with Stewart and Amanda fortunately was free to babysit.

On the dot of one o'clock, Stewart came out of the surgery building and spotted me immediately. He beckoned me over to his Jaguar and we drove off. As we neared his home, I had to crouch down in the car until we were safely in his garage with the door closed. The last thing we needed was for neighbours to see us. He asked me if I would like some lunch as he had the girls in his surgery buy some sandwiches, which were turkey with cranberry sauce and salmon with dill and cream cheese. Strangely enough, I wasn't hungry and neither was he, and so we put them in the fridge for later. His house was lovely and I found out that he had three children who had already broken up from a private school and gone away with their mother to England to see her family. I found it hard to believe that he was forty-three and I was only twenty-eight, but somehow I felt very comfortable with the age difference and after all, he was only two years older than Stan.

He led me into his daughter's bedroom and then proceeded to make love to me in every conceivable position that was possible. I was absolutely amazed as I really had only ever heard of the missionary position and had never known about oral sex until the other week. Then I couldn't believe it when he wanted to have a sixty-nine. I was a bit apprehensive as I had never thought about having that part of a man in my mouth yet when I tried it, I found it to be quite natural and very exciting. It was a wonderful feeling, satisfying each other at the same time in this way. Everything we did brought us closer together and we realised that our special love was becoming stronger.

It was a beautiful afternoon and I never wanted to it end but of course, time soon ran out. As we ate the sandwiches, I joked and asked him if he would like me to make him that cup of tea that he had had to decline last time at my house. He was amused and smiled and ended up making a cuppa in his kitchen for both of us.

I couldn't help thinking how thoughtful this marvellous man was to me, in every way.

Chapter 14

What Now?

On the afternoon of Friday 17th December, I arrived at Travancore with Paul and my honeymoon case full of clothes for him, which would last a week, not just three nights. I liked to buy Paul and Hayden expensive clothes as I wanted them to always look their best and the lady in the local children's wear shop was sure of a big sale whenever I went in there.

Matron Wilson was very sweet to me and told me not worry about Paul and to have a good break. I explained that we were going to Rosebud the next day and taking Hayden with us so that we could focus fully on him for a change. Then she said that she would be there at Travancore tomorrow for most of the day and would make a point of keeping an eye on him.

There was only one thing that worried me. The gates of the grounds were wide open. So I asked her if they were ever closed. The matron, or Edna, as she told me to call her, just laughed and said that the children were always supervised and never went near the front entrance as their playground area at the back was fully fenced. I cautioned her and said that Paul was a real force to be reckoned with when it came to running away. But she assured me that her staff had been briefed by Dr Patterson and knew what they were dealing with. Again, she stressed that everything would be all right and told me to make the most of some well-earned, worry-free sleep and hopefully have some enjoyable times with Stan and Hayden. She was such a lovely lady and I could tell that she really knew what I was going through. I was so grateful that she really wanted to help me.

That night, I had the best sleep I'd had for five years! I found that at last, I'd had a little bit of energy. The whole house seemed unusually quiet and peaceful but on the other hand, it felt rather strange not to be on duty all the time with Paul and of course, Hayden, at two and a half years old, had been no trouble at all.

It was about nine o'clock next morning when we finished loading everything into Stan's new Ford Coupe Falcon and set off for Rosebud. I was quite excited and put the car radio on and settled down to relax listening to an Abba song while Stan drove. We were just nearing Dromana when the record on radio station 3UZ finished and an urgent police message was broadcast.

My blood ran cold as I heard the announcer say that a five-year-old boy was missing from the Travancore Clinic and from the description that he gave, I knew it was Paul. I ordered Stan to stop at the next public phone booth and rushed inside to ring Edna. I was shaking and found it hard to get any words out but managed to tell her what we had just heard on the radio. She was very relaxed and said, 'Do not worry, dear. It isn't Paul who is missing. It's another little boy.'

I couldn't help but argue with her and said, 'The clothing they mentioned was Paul's.'

She seemed a bit embarrassed and said, 'You had brought so many clothes for Paul, they did not think you would mind lending one of Paul's outfits to another child who did not have enough clothes with him. Don't worry, just have a happy weekend.'

I wasn't entirely convinced but I felt helpless and so I politely thanked her and hung up. Stan was annoyed about the whole thing and said that I had overreacted and so we drove on to Rosebud in silence.

I felt a lot better when we arrived at the old house and I got out of the car to open the big wire gate with the name *Wenona* on it. I wanted to give Hayden the chance to experience some of my best childhood memories and I took great delight in showing him inside. I turned the power and the hot water on as I had done many times before and my mind went back to all the happy holidays I had had there. Somehow, it wasn't quite the same without all the family and also I noticed some minor alterations had been done to the house but the smell of the cedar exposed beans and the quiet ambience was still there as I remembered. I felt I was home again and nothing could harm me.

We had lunch at the large table where I had had so many unforgettable meals. Then I suddenly remembered 'the snake in the jam jar trick' and rushed to the sideboard cupboard. To my surprise, it was still there but the label looked very old and faded. I asked Hayden to unscrew the jar and *smell the jam* and a new snake, with a more powerful spring and different coloured cover, sprang out at him and he screamed with delight. Then he wanted me to smell the jam next time and get a fright, again and again, until I told him to try and trick his father.

After lunch, we went down to the boatshed. The double doors had been painted pale blue, covering the old green colour but apart from that, just about everything looked the same and it still had the salty, dank smell that I loved. My little dinghy was there but Stan was not interested in taking it out. I had a lovely time with Hayden and we lost no time in shedding our shoes. It felt so good to walk in the smooth fine sand again and little Hayden squealed joyously.

Stan was not really a beach person and was busy sitting in a deck chair reading the real estate section of the paper, so Hayden and I went for a paddle. After that, we built a sand castle. Then we went collecting shells, putting them in his plastic bucket, which was so much better than the old rusty, metal ones Sue and I had had to put up with.

The day ended happily as for the first time, I had had plenty of time to be a proper mother to my younger child. I decided to go to bed early and take advantage of another long, uninterrupted sleep. Stan said that he did not mind as he had a lot of paperwork to attend to and that he would probably be up most of the night anyway. I heaved a silent sigh of relief as the last thing I wanted was to be intimate with him.

I went to bed thinking how strange it was to be sleeping in the double bed where Auntie Beth and Uncle Bill had slept for as long as I could remember. It had a big hollow in the middle of the mattress and I was not surprised as I knew they had always been a very happy couple. As I fell asleep, I heard the old clock on the mantel piece in the lounge room chime nine o'clock and my thoughts went back to the old childhood feeling I used to have of safety and love whenever I stayed at *Wenona*. They were still there inside me after all this time.

Next day, we left Rosebud early and Stan had a shower at home, got changed, had a quick breakfast with us and went to work. Although refreshed and rejuvenated, I still felt a bit uneasy about leaving Paul at Travancore after the fright we had had the day before. I was not completely convinced it hadn't been Paul that had been lost and so I was determined to get him back home earlier and rang Travancore to tell them we were coming.

When we got there, a young girl had him ready for me and she said, 'What a good thing the police found Paul yesterday! The little monkey climbed down about thirty or more feet – ten metres – into the excavation pit for the new block of units' underground garage being built across the road. It took the police hours to find him!'

I was horrified and reached out to hug him but of course, he pushed me away.

All the way home, in the car, I was seething and I wondered why Edna had lied to me on the phone. The main thing, of course, was that Paul was all right but it could have easily been the other way round. I didn't know whether to tell Stan or not but halfway home, I decided not to as it was now in the past and I knew that I would receive no sympathy for something that he would see indirectly as my fault for wanting him to stay there in the first place. I started to feel panicky and all the good work of the two nights' uninterrupted sleep and relaxation was wearing off, fast. I was so worried and scared as to what would happen next. I now had nowhere for Paul to go as I was certain after this episode at Travancore they would not want him back again. I would be his keeper for life *but who could help me?*

I immediately felt quite sick and realised that I would never be free to go anywhere without Paul in the future. I probably would never be able to see Stewart alone again and I was so upset that I quietly sobbed as I drove all the way home. I felt as if I was back in prison for life and this time, there was no way out.

It was the Sunday before Christmas and Sue came down to see me alone. I had phoned her urgently as I needed someone to talk to. Mum had been flat out and luckily, this time preferred to stay home. Sue was still busy at her holiday job at Tim the Toy Man, a toy shop in the city, up until Christmas Eve. She had finished at Clyde School and her plan was to go back to university the following year and complete her Bachelor of Arts degree. I was so pleased to see her as distance had made it impossible for her to visit me outside school holidays and I had missed her so much. She looked so attractive with her hair in a French roll and she had really grown up. I couldn't believe that she would be twenty-three in February next year, which would be 1971, and I wondered where the years had gone!

She was a little awe-struck when she saw me lock us all in the house but soon saw why as Paul still displayed his usual bizarre behaviour. She sat down and halfway through her cup of tea, I decided to tell her about Stewart. To my great surprise, she did not criticise me and actually defended me, saying that she knew that things had never been good between Stan and I and that everyone deserved happiness. I was so relieved and hugged her madly and then I had a little weep.

I told her that I needed to see Stewart again and tell him what had happened but I could not speak to him properly with Paul screaming and wrecking the surgery. So, without thinking twice, she agreed to come down and stay with us for week or two after Christmas. This would enable me to be with the man that I loved and receive the comfort and support that I so desperately needed. I was so grateful and I loved her so much. In my heart, I hoped that one day I could do something just as wonderful for her. That afternoon, I had talked the leg off a chair and when I had finished, I eagerly said that it was her turn. My little sister smiled quizzically and I treasured being able share our inner most thoughts and special secrets.

Christmas came and went without any great celebrations as in our house every day was the same with a child like Paul to care for. The only memorable thing was for me to see was the look on Hayden's face when he found his presents from Santa. Of course, Paul was not forgotten but it was difficult to know what to give him as he was not interested in playing with toys, only destroying them. He delighted in ripping up any wrapping paper and boxes he could find and the house was a real mess.

Sue came down on Boxing Day and I was so glad to see her. Stan, of course, was out at his display home village and so we had a lovely time together. It was so good to have someone to talk to, especially when I was bathing the boys. They both loved the water but unfortunately, Hayden had learnt from Paul how to splash all the water out of the bath every night so poor Sue had to sit outside the bathroom door to avoid being drenched, like I was, every afternoon.

She had brought a bottle of McWilliam's Cream Sherry and we indulged in a glass or two, so mopping up the mess did not seem as tedious as usual. Sue had also brought some of the leftovers from Mum's Christmas dinner and so we had a most enjoyable meal in between springing into action every two minutes or so to rescue Paul from hurting himself.

I explained that I had made an appointment to see Stewart the next day and then the week after, I had to see Shane again. Sue said that she could look after Paul and Hayden but only for tomorrow and was sorry but she would only be able to stay for two days more as she wanted to give Mum a chance to get away. She had offered to fill in for her at one of the boutiques so that Mum and Dad could have a holiday at the Warburton Chalet. I was glad that she was in a position to help Mum, as I knew that I would never be able to do so and Mum badly needed a rest.

Next day, I was so grateful that Sue was able to mind my boys. The doctors' surgery was full of people after the Christmas break and I hoped that my consultation with Stewart would not be too long for Sue's sake. Nevertheless, I decided to make the most of it as it would be the last one without Paul by my side.

As I went into Stewart's room, I could see that he was ill at ease and I asked him what was wrong. He said, 'As we haven't been able to see each since your weekend away with Stan, I couldn't help thinking that maybe you both might have got back together again.'

I was dismayed and said, 'No! That is not the case. All it did was to make me feel that my marriage was well and truly over.'

I wondered how he could ever think of such a thing but on the other hand, it showed that he really cared about me. So I told him the whole story about Paul absconding from Travancore and that

I could only come to see him with Paul in tow in the future. He understood and became very remorseful.

'I just could not bear it if I lost you but I wonder how we are going to cope with everything. In my case, divorce is out of the question because of my profession. It would be frowned upon by the Australian Medical Association and my partners and so it would jeopardise my whole career.'

Of course, I knew that I had nowhere to go if I got a divorce, so we were both mystified as what to do.

We had a real problem and there was no solution. We both felt so sad and our eyes were tearing up.

There was only one thing left to do and that was to make passionate love right there in the surgery, which possibly would be for the very last time.

Chapter 15

Stops and Starts

A week later, Paul and I went to Travancore to see Dr Patterson. We were the first appointment for the day so luckily did not have to wait in the waiting room. I held my son's hand tightly and we marched in. Shane was polite and pleasant as usual and then got right to the point. He said, 'The matron and I were appalled at how bad Paul's symptoms really are. Just like at the autistic school, our staff here had never seen a child that was Profoundly Autistic before and the report they have given us is not very good.' Then there was a knock on the door and the matron let herself in.

I flew at Edna and asked, 'Why did you deny that Paul was lost when I phoned you the other day?'

She and Shane seemed very surprised that I had found out what had happened. Then Edna said, 'I didn't want to interrupt your holiday, dear, as I knew you were absolutely exhausted and that, as we were speaking on the phone, I had a signal from a member of staff that Paul had been found safe and well.'

I apologised to her profusely and then burst into tears. It was all becoming too much to bear. Paul seized the moment and broke away from me, running off with the doctor's prescription pad, ripping the pages into shreds and stuffing them into his mouth. I rushed to restrain him and Edna buzzed for a nurse to come and look after him while we finished the consultation. She went on to say, 'We are both very worried as we know that Paul is too much for you to manage on my own.' Then she asked a personal question. 'Have you and your husband managed to come closer again?'

I opened my heart and said, 'Absolutely not! Right from the start, I have had no real support from Stan as far as Paul is concerned. I just can't take it anymore and feel the marriage is over for me but I have nowhere to go.'

I started crying again and they both said that they wanted to help me.

Edna suggested that Paul be put into their residential care at Travancore for weekdays and come home for the weekends for a trial period. Naturally, I was still a bit sceptical and Edna read my thoughts. She smiled and said, 'Paul would be safe as he would have someone with him at all times and be in a special secured area.'

Then Shane said, 'I will be here during the week also if I am needed for any reason.' Their offer sounded wonderful and I was so thankful that I gave Edna a big hug.

All the way home, I felt like a different person. There was light at the end of the tunnel. I was going to be able to sleep again, normally, next week. How marvellous. I thought what an amazing morning I had had. Things were not that bad after all. I thanked God and couldn't wait to tell Stewart.

That night when Stan arrived home at 11.45 p.m, I told him what was happening and he seemed quite pleased about it as both of us had been sleep deprived for so long. Then he quickly changed the subject and became very excited and said, 'I have some really exciting news. I've decided to leave my job and start my own building and investment company with three of my Terra Firma mates as silent partners. We are looking at an old inner-city shop to use as an office and I am certain that this move will set me "on the road to riches!"'

However, after my huge day, I found it difficult to be concerned about anything like this and fell asleep in the middle of what he was saying.

During the next six weeks, quickies – as I found out was the name – happened with Stewart and me in the surgery once a week. The problem was that the more we had, the more we wanted, so then it became twice a week. Even though Paul was in residential care, seeing one another, in this way, still wasn't the perfect solution. In my heart, I wanted to marry Stewart. I loved him and wanted to be by his side forever and most of all, legally. I did not want to have to make an appointment to see him all the time and so one day, I asked him, straight out, what would happen if he did get a divorce.

He looked sad and frustrated, and said, 'I have been thinking about it constantly. I am deeply concerned that I would not know how I could adequately support my ex-wife and three teenagers, who will all be at boarding school next year, as well as you and your two children. Also as I have said before, the Australian Medical Association would almost certainly take a dim view of it and my reputation would be damaged. I would most likely have no choice but to give up my place in the medical practice as it would not be fair for the other doctors to have a disgraced partner.'

We both looked at each other and felt hopelessly thwarted by the whole situation. Our relationship was unbelievably wonderful but also bitter-sweet. It was driving us both crazy. Before I left, Stewart offered me a free sample packet of a new anti-depressant drug and he said that he was going to try it as well.

On other free times of the weeks, I threw myself into my work and opened up an extra office in Camberwell. I found Carmel Callaghan, a very well-spoken, mature lady, to run it for me and was amazed at its instant success. We actually had walk-in business off the street as the main window faced a main road and the sign which an old friend had made for me. It read Sadie's Ladies, complete with artwork of mops and buckets that said it all. Stan was thrilled with my efforts and had actually helped me paint and fit out the tiny office space. I was pleasantly surprised and thankful as he knew that I could not have afforded it otherwise.

Unfortunately, the weekends came around very quickly and I found myself dreading them. I felt so guilty but all the strength that I had gained from having normal sleep during the week suddenly flowed out of me when Paul had to come home. In the back of my mind, I was still fearful of what the future had in store for me and my poor little boy. I also wondered if Paul, being Profoundly Autistic, was also another barrier to Stewart not getting a divorce. I didn't think it was but I would not have blamed him as Paul was not getting any better and still, there was no cure. I got depressed thinking about it so I started taking the free tablets and hoped that I would feel better. After three days, my face had blown up like a football. I could hardly see out of my eyes as they had become slits in amongst a puffy face. I was horrified and rushed down to the surgery. The girls on the front desk gasped in amazement and as Stewart called out my name, it was my turn to be amazed. Stewart's face had blown up as well!

In a day or so, the side effects were subsiding. We joked about how the anti-depressant tablets had made us both look very much like Japanese sumo wrestlers. Then as we got our normal faces back, we felt marvellous and I reminded Stewart that I was taking Valium. He said that he was also and that the drug that we had taken must not have been compatible with it.

However, a few weeks later, he found another drug, which he had tested on himself and so far, there had been no adverse reactions, so I decided to try it also. We were both desperate and getting more depressed about our future every day as we realised that the odds were stacked against us.

I had no idea at this stage that I was on the verge of becoming hooked on prescription drugs.

The months were flying by. Soon, it was November and Paul turned six. Apart from all my dramas during the year, two other major things had happened in our family. Firstly, Sue had been contacted just before school started by her old English teacher and mentor from MLC, our old school. She persuaded Sue to defer from university for another year and join her teaching at Toorak College, Mount Eliza, where she had just become the new head mistress. Sue loved it. It was good for me also, as sometimes she popped in for a meal. Secondly, Mum had opened another shop in the Mount Eliza Village and so now with three shops, she was doing very well and I saw her a bit more.

I was at my Mount Eliza office, with Olive Cooper, when I received a phone call from Edna at Travancore. Immediately, she told me not to worry as Paul was fine. She just wanted to make an appointment for me to come and see her the following week. We decided that the next Monday morning would be best when I could take Paul back there again after his weekend at home. I asked her why she wanted to see me and she said that she had something important to tell me but she wanted to tell me face to face. I knew her well enough to know that it was not going to be good news and so I made sure that I kept on with my antidepressant capsules.

On Monday, Edna had tea and warm jam and cream scones brought to her office for us and Shane, who had joined us.

She said, 'There is no way I can break what I have to say to you gently, my dear. I have received a rap over the knuckles from my superiors for letting Paul stay for over two months in the residential wing during weekdays and nights. The accommodation that I am in charge of is only supposed to be for temporary cases, like the first weekend when you went to Rosebud. Shane and I have tried to help you but the present arrangement cannot go on. The department has found out that Paul has overstayed and is adamant that he leave at the end of this month, which is in ten days.'

There were endless tears from me. I felt as if I was at the end of the road. Edna and Shane were very sympathetic and I asked them what on Earth I could do.

Edna said, 'I have written a letter of introduction for you to see Mrs Madeline Swanson, who is the matron of the Kew Cottages.' Shane handed me a referral.

In those days, the Children's Cottages at Kew had a terrible name. They were situated on the grounds of an adult lunatic asylum, where the insane were put away and forgotten forever. I remembered laughing with my friends on the bus going past the place to school as someone pointed and called it the loony bin. There were often disturbing articles in the newspapers and programs on television about the Cottages, with footage showing derelict buildings in need of repair with some poor little Mongoloid (now known as Down's Syndrome) children crowded inside in unhygienic conditions. The thought of Paul going there made me nearly vomit up my morning tea. I was frozen with fear and could not believe their suggestion.

Edna said kindly, 'You should go out there as soon as possible and meet Matron Swanson and form your own opinion, as it is not like you imagine it to be.'

I was in a complete state of shock but I realised that both Edna and Shane had gone beyond their normal boundaries to help me and in doing so, had risked their jobs, so I knew that I had to trust their judgement. I thanked them and left for home, knowing that after ten days, I would never be returning to Travancore ever again.

I went straight to Stewart's surgery and by chance caught him as he was just finishing his morning appointments. Joanne, at reception, could see I was very upset and ushered me into his room as soon as she could. Stewart's face was filled with anguish as he listened to my tale of woe. He sympathised and said that he was so sorry but it seemed that there was nothing else he or anyone could do to help Paul at this point in time. He virtually said what Edna had said and urged me to reserve my judgement until I had seen Matron Swanson. I could tell by the look on his face that he was trying to remain positive and composed for my sake. Then I asked him how he would feel if it were one of his children who was going to be put in there and he could not look at me and stared into space with teary eyes.

I broke down and became hysterical and so he gave me an injection of Valium to settle me down. He put his arms around me and comforted me as best he could until the injection worked. Then he said, 'You have to be even braver than previously, Lynne, and I am sure that you can do it.'

I was so grateful for his empathy and deep concern and thanked him for taking care of me. He kissed me gently on the forehead, told me that he loved me and then kissed me lightly on the lips. Of course, I told him that I loved him too and that I would always love him, and would never forget the compassion that he had just shown me in my hour of need.

For once we did not feel like making love but there was no need to as this heart-wrenching experience had somehow cemented us together all the more.

I went out the door feeling a lot stronger as I knew that I was not alone in all of this.

There was no other choice left for me and so I had made up my mind to telephone Matron Swanson as soon as I got home.

Chapter 16

Things Are Not Always As They Seem

I had to wait until the following week before Matron Swanson could see me. By this time, I had pulled myself together, thanks to Stewart and the new anti-depressant drug I was taking with the Valium tablets. I had been able to convey to Mum and Stan what Matron Wilson and also Dr Patterson had said, making it clear that there were no more options left for Paul. Stan didn't want to talk about it. However, Mum said she was sorry that she was unavailable to come with me to meet Matron Swanson but said that she would firmly support me in whatever decision, I chose to make.

Madeleine Swanson was very businesslike. She had her hair in a strict bun at the back of her head and wore thin black-rimmed glasses. I was also so impressed with all her certificates on the wall. I could tell by her eyes that although she was an intellectual, she was also a down-to-earth person. I told her of my dilemma in great detail and she said that she was fully aware of the facts and had actually seen Paul at Travancore with one of her child psychiatrists the day before.

She offered to show me around the Cottages and I was dismayed at the lack of repairs to the buildings. It seemed like a forgotten part of the world that had been just left standing with nothing done to them, decaying for decades and quite inhabitable. My heart sank as I trembled and was close to tears but she explained that they would soon be demolished as a new unit housing block was due to be built soon for all the patients. I was relieved to hear that but like Mum, I was still wary.

She led me through to a cottage that had children in it about the same age as Paul and introduced me to the charge nurse. She was of Dutch origin and immediately, I knew that she was dedicated to the welfare of the children. She proudly showed me through her ward and I found it to be spotless. The wards were large rooms in each cottage, painted grey, with rows of beds for sleeping. Attentive staff tended to the day rooms furnished with a few small-sized tables and chairs, and a mattress for those who could not walk on the old wooden floors that smelt slightly of antiseptic.

The children were safe and as happy as they could be, considering that they all suffered varying degrees of different mental illnesses. They were clean and dressed in good-quality clothes and shoes. I knew in a flash that these children were fortunate to have such caring staff who all seemed to love them as individuals. I was really impressed. It was then that I made the most important decision of my life. I wanted Paul to be there! I knew that he would have a much better life than being with me. Also, I had to think of Hayden, who would at last have a chance at a normal life.

We went back to the office and Matron Swanson said that Paul had already been assessed as Profoundly Autistic, and was in need of permanent twenty-four-hour residential care and as a result, the Kew Cottages would accept him. I did not know whether to laugh or cry as the news seemed so final and yet I felt such great relief. Matron Swanson gave me some forms to fill in and said to send them to her as there was no hurry. I begged to differ as Paul had to leave Travancore the day after next and I was hoping that he could go straight there, so I eagerly signed the forms immediately. Matron Swanson looked at me sadly as if I did not understand the situation. Then, she dropped a bombshell.

'I am so sorry but there will not be a vacancy for three years.'

I was devastated!

'What would happen if I died in the next three years?' I cried, panic-stricken.

'Well, Lynne, of course, then we would have to find a place for him,' she said.

I had an appointment for four o'clock to see Stewart and I arrived at the surgery on the dot. I was in a state of disbelief. All the stress and strain about deciding whether or not Paul should go to the Kew Cottages had now faded into insignificance. It was now a question of how I could survive another three years with him at home full-time. It was an outcome I had not imagined and I was not sure how to handle it. Thank goodness I had Stewart to talk to.

A receptionist on the front desk was polite but said that unfortunately, I could not see Stewart. I couldn't believe what she had just said. I asked her why as I had an appointment. She just said that Dr Applegate was unavailable and if I would like to see one of the other partners, she would squeeze me in as she knew I was having a hard time with Paul. I made it clear that if I could not see my doctor, then I would see no one else and I stormed out of the door.

Once outside, I checked the doctor's car park and sure enough, Stewart's car was not there. I wondered where he was. Today of all days, I needed him urgently. It was unlike him not to tell me if he was going to away from the surgery and I became alarmed.

I did some shopping and then picked up Hayden from Eunice's daycare premises on the Nepean Highway. Then I went back to the medical centre and waited until the girls knocked off work and I saw my favourite receptionist, Joanne, walking to her car. I approached her and asked her to tell me where Stewart had gone. She was caught in a tight spot and I knew she felt sorry for me but of course, we both did not want her to lose her job. Then she said she would tell me in confidence, after looking around, that Dr Applegate had gone away somewhere but that was all she knew. In fact, he had been away from the day I had seen him last. She said that it seemed like some kind of closely guarded secret as to where he had gone but she would try to find out for me. I thanked her so much and was thankful that I had some kind of lead in this bizarre twist of fate. I could not help feeling sick with worry, not only for Paul and me but for Stewart also.

Where was he, and why hadn't he let me know where he had gone?

Hayden and I arrived home and there was an important letter waiting for me from Stewart's solicitor. I felt a chill go up my spine.

It said that he was acting for his client and that if I persisted in harassing Dr Stewart Applegate, then I would face court action. I had seven days to respond and in the event of no reply, legal action would take place.

This nearly finished me! I could not believe it! How could the man I love do this to me? I sat down and tried to understand why this was happening to me. All my love suddenly turned to anger but then back to love again. Why didn't my darling Stewart love me anymore? There was something strange about the whole thing but I had an even more pressing problem. I had to think of a way to help Paul and fast. That night I went to bed with a cocktail of Valium, antidepressants and sherry, and went out like a light.

Next day, I could feel the adrenalin rushing through my veins as I prepared for the fight of my life. Tomorrow Paul would have to leave Travancore and so I could not put it off any longer. I had to act right away. I swallowed a few more anti-depressants and then plucked up enough courage to phone Matron Swanson.

I did not take no for an answer when the girl on the switchboard told me that she was in a meeting and unavailable. I said that it was urgent and a life-and-death situation. Within seconds, Matron Swanson was on the line. I told her that there was no way I could have Paul home tomorrow to be with me for the next three years. I was too tired and had no strength left, and my spirit had been broken. I was so desperate that there was only one thing left that I could do. If the Kew Cottages would not take Paul tomorrow, then I would collect him from Travancore myself and kill us both.

The matron was very calm and asked how I proposed to do such a thing. I told her that I had thought it all out and that it would be very easy. As I had a sports car, I would drive as fast as I could down Oliver's Hill and instead of turning right at the bend in the road, go straight ahead and crash through the old wire fence on top of the cliff and land on the rocks and sink into the water below. Then she asked me who would look after Hayden. I told her that my mother would look after him and that she would understand why I had to do it and would forgive me so there was nothing left to stop me. There was a pause on the phone. Then Matron Swanson said not to do anything tomorrow and to stay home as there would be a letter from her coming in the mail. I was in such a state that I did not know what this meant but decided to agree to her wishes. I found myself thanking her for something that I was not sure of and hung up, thinking that at least I had done my best.

The next thing on my agenda was to see Joanne at the medical centre and find out what on Earth was happening with my beloved Stewart. It was nearly lunchtime when I arrived and I peeped through the glass door to look for Joanne. I saw a new older woman there with the other girls. She was overweight and did not wear fashionable clothes like the other girls in the surgery. Instead, she wore a well-worn white nurse's uniform that had seen better days, which focused all attention to her straight, bright, carrot-red hair. She seemed to be very forceful and ruling the roost. I could tell the others did not like her.

I waited until Joanne came out with the doctors' sandwich orders and I cornered her, just out of view of the surgery. After she had sworn me to secrecy, she said that she had found out that Dr Applegate was at the Melbourne private clinic at a seminar and that was all she knew. I thanked her and gave her a little hug. Then she inquired about Paul and I told her the story. As we parted, I asked her who the new bossy lady was behind the desk. Her eyes rolled back as she explained that that was Zelda, Dr Applegate's wife, who had been a trained nursing sister and had delighted in coming in now and giving them a hard time. She said that everyone hated Mrs Bossy Boots and wondered how long poor Dr Applegate could put up with her. Then she smiled at me and went on her way.

I arrived at the clinic at two-thirty in the afternoon, hoping that I might catch Stewart having an afternoon tea break at some time. I was surprised to see that it was actually a psychiatric clinic and had a residential section. I was still puzzled as to why he had not told me earlier that he was going there for the seminar and of course, more so about the letter. I went to reception and asked what time they would be having an afternoon tea break in the medical seminar being held there. The woman behind the counter looked at me as if I was mad and said coldly, 'What medical seminar?'

I suddenly realised that one did not exist and I apologised, saying that I must have the wrong place. I decided not to press my luck with her as I could tell by her attitude that she thought I must be one of their mental patients, hallucinating or something worse.

I went out of the main entrance but was determined not to give up. I followed the building along until I found another door, which opened into some kind of common room. A shy little lady was making herself a cup of tea with boiling water from an urn and asked me if I wanted one. I was very grateful as I had not had any lunch, and she also offered me a biscuit. She asked me when I had arrived and I realised that she thought I was a new patient, so I said that I was actually looking for a friend.

After a short discussion about nothing, I asked her if she knew a Dr Applegate and she said that she had never heard of him. I was starting to think that maybe I was on a wild goose chase when I asked her again but this time I said Stewart Applegate. Again, she said that she did not know of a Stewart Applegate but in her group therapy session there was a new man called Stu. I described him and she nodded her head, saying that he had an English accent. At long last, I was getting somewhere. Then I asked her their doctor's name and she said it was a Dr Norris. All of a sudden she didn't want to speak any more and ran out of the room. I followed her out into a passage. It had waiting rooms and doctor's names on the doors. Finally, as I was just about to give up, I saw the name Dr William Norris on the last door. I had just had some more tablets with the tea and I was feeling very confident, so I knocked on the door. A voice said to come in, so in I went.

I politely introduced myself to Dr Norris and I was quite amazed when he seemed to know who I was. I asked why Stewart was there and he said that he could not discuss anything about his patient with me. Then, I asked if I could see him and Dr Norris said that his patient did not want to see me, and *I could not believe it!*

Dr Norris obviously did not realise how close we were and I asked him again. He reiterated what he had just said and I became furious and said that I did not believe him. I could see that I was getting nowhere so I took a different tack. I asked him what exactly was wrong with Stewart and again, he refused to give out any information, saying that it was a confidential matter and as I was not his family, he could not divulge anything. Hearing that was like a red rag to a bull to me and I snapped. I shouted that I was more like his wife than the one he had and therefore I had some rights, and I demanded to see him.

'Perhaps if you come back tomorrow, he may see you then,' he said.

I could tell that I would never get anywhere with this painful person. I got up, opened the door and yelled out in the passage for everyone to hear, 'Tomorrow might be too late, Dr Norris. I may have to kill myself and my Profoundly Autistic son tomorrow and you won't even let me say goodbye to the only man I have truly loved in my whole life. You should be ashamed of yourself, calling yourself a doctor! You don't really care about people at all!'

I had really lost it and made a grand exit through the main entrance, with the bewildered doctor staring after me and the cold woman at the desk, slinging off at me, saying, 'Oh! No! Not you again. How did you get back in here?' So I ran to my car and sobbed uncontrollably for ten minutes before I could drive and collect Hayden. How I made it home, I shall never know.

The following day, I waited on tenterhooks for the postman to arrive and filled in the morning telephoning my offices and also talking to Amanda who was cleaning the house. In the back of my mind, I was still mulling over all of yesterday's amazing events and I decided not to think about the Kew Cottages until I received the matron's letter. However, I was still thinking about the episode at the psychiatric clinic and couldn't fathom it out. I was tempted to have some more pills but the way I was consuming my medication, I was going to run out soon so I made an appointment to see a new local doctor, Dr Walker, for the next morning.

Suddenly, the postman came with an express delivery letter and I tore it open. It was from the matron and it said that today, *Paul would be transported from the Travancore clinic to the Children's Cottages at Kew as a permanent resident.* I was so relieved but part of me also felt guilty. I lay down on the bed and cried, rocking the whole bed with my tears of relief and sadness. I took some more pills and soon felt better, and then rang Mum and told her what had happened. She was glad that I was satisfied that the best outcome for Paul had been reached and we made plans for us to visit him together on Sunday.

The next call I made was to Matron Swanson and I thanked her with all my heart and she said, 'Sometimes rules are meant to be broken in special cases, Lynne, and as far as I could see, this was one of them.'

I let her know that Mum and I would be out to visit Paul on Sunday and she was very pleased. Then she told me that Paul had arrived in the morning and that he was settling in well, and all the staff in his cottage ward had fallen in love with him. I thanked her again, and she told me to look after myself.

I thanked God that Paul had been taken care of for life and now the only thing left was to tell Stan when he came home. It was very late and he replied in a loud bad-tempered voice.

'I hope you're happy now, Lynne, because you have just given our son away!'

Chapter 17

It Was Now or Never

The next morning, I was still upset at Stan's vicious words. He had known that Paul would become a ward of the state and I felt bad enough without having to put up with a reaction like that. I wanted support and I wanted love at this stressful time. I felt as if I had a knife in my back and one in my heart. How I longed for the only man who could give me what I needed most but why had Dr Norris at the clinic said that Stewart did not want to see me? It was definitely not like the Stewart I knew – or thought I knew. What was wrong with him and why had Stewart sent me that terrible legal letter? I was just starting to think that I had better acknowledge it when I heard Stan's raised voice from the kitchen. In all of the worry of yesterday, I had forgotten to hide the letter from Stewart's solicitor and had left it beside the one from Matron Swanson on the bench and now Stan had found it. He asked me if there was a reason why it had been sent to me and I replied honestly that I did not know and it had come as a complete surprise.

All at once, Stan started dictating a letter of reply for me to type. It was not really the kind of letter that I would have written, though.

It started off accusing the writer of making false statements and threats. Then the rest of the letter made it look like that his client was the one who had been harassing me and had therefore been guilty of professional misconduct. The final sentence said that if it continued, then I would make a formal complaint to the Australian Medical Association and that I would also take legal action.

I had no choice but to type the letter and to sign it. Then Stan said, almost gloatingly, 'I will save you the trouble of posting it and will post it myself on the way to work.'

There was nothing I could do. I felt yet another knife pierce my heart. What had I just done? I was a nervous wreck and finished off the last of my tablets.

Dr Hugh Walker filled in my new patient card as I related all my problems with Paul and my marriage. He asked me why I had come to him and not my usual doctor, Dr Applegate. I explained that my doctor had gone away and his surgery could not tell me when he would be back and that I did not like any of the other partners. He was very nice and seemed to understand how I was feeling and what I had gone through, even though I had not told him a word about my personal relationship with Stewart. He gave me new scripts for my medications and told me to try and have a complete rest whilst I came to terms with having to place Paul in the Cottages. Then he said if my depression got worse to ring him immediately.

On Sunday, Mum and I went out to see Paul. We were both apprehensive at first but luckily, the Dutch charge nurse, Sister Lara Van Der Berg, was on duty and welcomed us with open arms. Mum, like me, was immediately impressed at her warmth and love for all the children, and then we saw Paul, dressed in brand new clothes, happily bouncing on a trampoline, watched by a young nurse enjoying his laughter. We had never seen Paul so happy before and it was a load off our minds. Then Mum agreed that I had certainly made the right decision.

I was so pleased to have Mum's approval. Of course, she had no idea the obstacles I had had to overcome to get Paul admitted to the Cottages and I never wanted her to know. However, she did know that I was mentally and physically exhausted and so she offered to take Hayden home with her and have him for as long as I needed. Also, there was a new pre-kindergarten child-minding centre that had opened up nearby that he could attend during the day. I was so thankful and relieved as I just felt like collapsing into a heap. Then I confessed that my marriage was on the rocks and she said that she was well aware of it and would always support me. I thought how lucky I was to have a mother like that and was amazed at how well she knew me.

The following day, I found it strange to be in a house without any children that needed me and so I decided to go to my Mount Eliza office and get back into the swing of things. The medication was slowing me down but I still knew what I was doing. I went up the stairs and was surprised to find that the office was closed. I unlocked the door and to my disbelief, I found that my files had been taken from the filing cabinets and the office abandoned. I was so upset as I had trusted Olive. I knew in a flash, that most likely she had started up her own agency and taken all my clients. It was unbelievable as I had had complete faith in her.

Fear and anxiety set in as I phoned the Camberwell office and got no reply. So I phoned Carmel at her home and she answered the phone, saying, 'Housework Helpers'. I asked her why she had done this to me and she said that she was tired of doing all the work while I was swanning around in a flashy sports car, not bothering to visit her for weeks on end. After hearing that, I was so upset and asked her about Olive Cooper. It seemed that they had put their heads together and milked me out of my business.

Before I hung up, I said to her, 'I can't believe that you both would do this to me.'

Then she said, proudly, 'My wealthy husband will fight you if you choose to take it further.'

I couldn't take much more. My life was a nightmare!

I came home and against my better judgement, I decided to ring Dr Norris, whom I did not trust, to see if Stewart was ready to see me yet. The doctor was very abrupt and said, 'By now, you should have received a letter from my patient's solicitor and so you have to understand that Dr Applegate never wants to see you or speak to you ever again.'

I was so hurt but I summoned up enough courage to ask why. The doctor said, 'You have to face up to reality, Lynette. Compared to his wife and children, you will always be second best.'

Mortified, I hung up and went straight for the bottles of my drugs, which were full. I was starting to wonder if Stewart ever had really loved me after all. He seemed to have suddenly slipped out of my life and no one, including him, it appeared, wanted me to be near him. I did not want to die, even though I felt like it, but I really needed something to dull the pain. In desperation, I phoned Dr Walker and asked him how many tablets I could take for me to sleep a whole week.

As instructed by him, I quickly packed a bag and within five minutes, a taxi had arrived at the door and I was driven to a private Peninsula hospital. Dr Walker was waiting for me and led me into a pretty room with a sea view and then he asked me to hand over all my medication. He looked at the contents in the bottles and then gave it all to a nurse and was very pleasant and said that he knew I was tired. He told me that I could stay there and relax for at least a week or longer. Then he went outside while I changed into my nightie and got into bed. When he came back, I thanked him and he gave me an injection. As I was floating off, he said, 'Try not to worry now as I will telephone Stan and your mother for you.'

When I woke up, it was early evening and I suddenly remembered where I was. It was lovely not having to worry about anything. A nurse came in with a delicious roast chicken dinner and I was surprised that I ate it all and actually enjoyed it. Later on, I was looking forward to a cup of coffee so I got my new container of sugar substitute tablets out of my beauty case. I only needed to take half of one and as they were hard to break, I used the knife that I had kept off the food tray to cut them into two. I ended up with about sixty little white half tablets on my tray table and was just about to put them back into the plastic cylinder when all of a sudden two nurses came in and seized me by the arms, and then confiscated the sweeteners. I laughed out loud as I explained to them what they were and that I only took half of one in my cup of coffee. Nevertheless, they said that they were only following orders and did not give them back. They also took the knife and I couldn't help overhearing one nurse whisper to the other that I 'had to be watched at all times'. It sounded a bit drastic to me as I knew that there was nothing really wrong with me. I just needed a long sleep.

Two weeks later, I felt so much better after all the years of sleep deprivation I had suffered. I was allowed to sit by myself in the sun in the rear garden for small interludes so I had plenty of time to think about my future. I decided that I had to do something that I liked as for years I had not really done anything just for me. Then

I thought of taking up singing professionally again. I remembered the times as a teenager I had sung on TV in a daytime show called *Thursday at One* on Channel 9. So I started softly singing one of my songs from music in my practice cassette player that Gloria, my singing teacher, had taught me and was alarmed and dismayed. I had lost my singing voice. It sounded terrible so I knew that I would have to find a new teacher as Gloria had retired.

Next, I would have to divorce Stan.

I felt that Mum would not mind if I rented the flat at back of one of her shops with Hayden and hopefully worked for her.

The only thing that I could not solve was how to forget Stewart and deep down, I knew that I would never forget him.

I was still puzzling about the whole situation when I heard Dr Walker talking behind the hedge in the garden to the hospital matron.

They didn't realise I was there and I heard him say, 'Lynette is coming along really well. She should be able to go home soon. Incidentally, I found out why Dr Applegate, her previous doctor, was unavailable for her to see. He was in a private psychiatric clinic, suffering from a severe nervous breakdown similar to hers!'

Oh! I had not realised that I was so ill until I heard what Dr Walker had just said. Also, I was completely unaware that Stewart was also suffering the same fate. How he had ever sanctioned that letter from his solicitor to me was still a mystery. But now, of course, I was just as bad as I had been made to reply to it in a manner that was also out of character for me and I hated myself for playing into Stan's hands. Unfortunately, I knew that I was too weak to fight any more and I thought that Stewart could be feeling the same way.

Suddenly, it had become all too much for me and I decided to make a mammoth decision and that was to erase Stewart from my mind as he had been forced to do with me.

I cried that night until the nurse came in and gave me a strong sedative.

The next day, Dr Walker came to see me and asked me when I would be ready to go home. I said, 'I will be ready in two days as I know that I just have to come to terms with plans I have made for myself and need a bit more time to adjust.'

After two days, Stan came to the hospital and drove me home. It should have been a joyous event but we both knew that our marriage was over. I told Stan that I would be moving out with Hayden soon and gave him the address of where I was going to live.

He was seething and put his foot down on the accelerator and sped for five minutes but this could hardly contain his thunderous, rapid rage. He bellowed, 'Don't expect me to be there when you move out!'

He said to let him know when I would be going as he did not want to be there when the removalist van came. I realised that he had been controlling me in a cruel, negative way, but I was now sick and tired of it and I could not wait to get rid of him and his manipulation. I had come to a decision and that was to get on with my life, with my dear little Hayden.

The move went without a hitch. I only took bare essentials as the flat behind the shop was partly furnished.

However, I felt extremely sad as I walked out the front door for the last time and realised what I had lost.

In seven years, I had lost my husband, my elder son, my lover, my business, my house and my health.

But at least I had survived!

Chapter 18

Twists & Turns

I moved into the residence at the back of one of Mum's shops just up the road from her home but she wisely said that Hayden should stay with her until I was back on my feet. I was so lucky to have her and I will never forget what she did for me. Thank goodness that I didn't have Hayden with me on the first night as I was woken up by being invaded by a group of mice crawling all over my bed and trying to burrow into my long hair! The shop's flat had been empty for a long time and so they must have been looking for food. *Yuck!*

A few days later, I painted the whole of the interior, carpeted it and tried to make a fresh start.

It was 1972 and I was thirty. Gough Whitlam had just become Prime Minister so I was grateful that there was now a single mother's pension that would help support me financially. But unfortunately, I had lost confidence in myself and had become almost a social recluse. It was so bad that for the first week, I stayed in bed most mornings until late when I felt I could face a new day. I only got up to go shopping for food and/or to renew my prescription for Valium as Dr Walker had gradually taken me off the anti-depressants.

Then one day, I received a letter from Stan's solicitor.

Stan was filing for custody of Hayden!

The thought of Stan having custody of Hayden shocked me into immediate action. I had to get out from under the dark cloud that I was under. Then I remembered what I had thought of in the hospital to cheer me up and bring me back to life again. I had to now get my singing voice back so I made a time for a lesson with the nearest singing teacher I could find.

His name was Sebastian Starr and I had vaguely heard of him, a long time ago. He had a vacancy that morning so I went to his studio but I was feeling very shy and inadequate. Seb, as he said to call him, opened the door and looked as if he was about to go on stage. He wore beautifully tailored clothes and an expensive gold chain around his neck. He shook hands and I noticed gold rings with huge diamonds on each hand like the American pianist Liberace wore. I was quite fascinated. He was about twenty-five years older than I was but there was something about him that I liked. Then he asked me for my sheet music, which luckily I still had, and he started playing one of my songs on his grand piano, which had a beautiful chandelier hanging above it. He played it so well that I knew that I would enjoy my lesson. Unfortunately, when I tried to sing, I could not sing properly. I was so ashamed and embarrassed of my voice. I was slurring all the words and had no control over them. They would not sound how my brain wanted them to and to make matters worse, it spoilt Seb's wonderful accompaniment.

He looked at me in a fatherly way and asked me to tip out the contents of my handbag. I was startled by the request but he added that if I wanted to get my voice back then I may need to kick the habit I had. I was so taken aback that he had detected my problem. To my amazement, he took my bottle of Valium and marched me off to the toilet where he flushed all the tablets away in front of me. I was horrified but he said that as he was a reformed alcoholic, it was the only way to go. Then he asked for any repeat prescriptions that I had and ripped them up. I was speechless and wondered why I had let a complete stranger do this. Seb said that the next twenty-four hours would be very tough but I would be okay. He was firm and said, 'You certainly will *not* be okay if you keep on the way that you are going.' I tried to tell him about how I became the way I was but he was not interested.

He said, 'I am only interested in helping you regain your voice and your life.'

Deep down, I knew that he was right and felt at long last there was someone at this moment in my life who really understood what was going on with me and what mattered the most: *how to help me.*

As the days went by, with Seb's help, I won the battle against Valium.

My singing voice had returned and I was so grateful to him.

A theatrical agent wanted a publicity photo and soon I had regular Saturday night bookings. My dreams had come true and I was so happy.

I had stars in my eyes!

However, one day I started feeling really tense again, as the custody case for Hayden was going to be the next day. Seb comforted me and said, 'There is no need to worry as it is natural to be concerned. All you need is to relax and have a massage.'

I had never had one before and as I trusted him, I let him go ahead. It felt so good and I told him that I did not want him to stop, so he didn't. The therapeutic massage suddenly turned into foreplay and I was once again whisked away by a charming man on a magic carpet ride to outer space. He was an expert lover and the whole thing had seemed like a theatrical production. I went home feeling that I could face anything the next day.

My lawyer, Mrs Somerfield, was very smart and completely on my side. I was overjoyed when she rang and said that *I had WON the case.* Hayden was not going to live with his father, only having weekend visits when it suited both parties. After telling the good news to Mum, I rushed off to see Seb. He was delighted and we celebrated with a lemon squash and a quick cuddle as he had pupils coming that afternoon after school.

The only thing left to worry about were the legal fees. I hoped that it would not take all my savings. As an investment, I owned a block of land at Rye Back Beach that I had bought for three hundred pounds when I was working at the insurance company. I had paid it off on terms for three years and it was probably now worth about two thousand dollars. It was in the middle of sand dunes with just a sandy track to it, and very hard to find. It would be years before the area ever went ahead. Luckily for me, I did not have to sell it as the solicitor's and barrister's fees were more reasonable than I had imagined.

I was now feeling very happy and well, and I realised how being drugged all the time had had a dangerous effect on me. I was free at last and asked Mum if I could come and work for her part-time to fit in with my pension, and she said that she would love to have me and show me the ropes. I began working the following day and she handed me a straw broom. She said that in order to succeed in the rag trade, I had to start at the bottom and that was to sweep the footpath first thing every day outside the shop on Toorak Road. I liked all aspects of the business but most of all when we went on buying trips to Flinders Lane and were shown the latest fashion ranges for the next season. I had even thought I might have some fashion parades one day as I knew I could compare them.

I still had time for my singing lessons but one day I was very surprised when Seb told me that he was in danger of losing his grand piano. It appeared that for some reason, he had been trying to establish himself again after a financial setback and the piano was on hire purchase. He had missed a few payments and they were coming to repossess it the next day. I was so shocked and immediately felt sorry for him. He said that he needed to borrow about a thousand dollars to pay it off and some other debts and could I help him with a loan? I said that I didn't have that much money in the bank but I would find it for him. I realised that I had developed a deep affection for this man even though he was old enough to be my father. He had saved me from my drug addiction and so what else could I do? Money could not buy what he had done for me.

So I sold my block of land easily to a real estate agent in Rye and he gave me two cheques as I requested. One was made out to Sebastian Starr for one thousand dollars and one for me for one thousand dollars.

Seb was thrilled and promised to pay me back as soon as he could. Unfortunately, it did not stop there and I discovered as time went by that my hand was always in my pocket and no money was ever paid back to me. I found it difficult to refuse him as I seemed to be under his spell and didn't want to disappoint him.

This went on for a few more months and I noticed that one by one, things started to go missing. The grand piano had gone and was replaced by an old organ, which was fine but I thought I had saved it. I couldn't help wanting to know what had happened but I didn't want to confront him about it. Next, I noticed the chandelier and his expensive jewellery except for one ring had also disappeared.

One Saturday afternoon, as I was locking up Mum's shop, I saw him coming out of the nearby TAB with a transistor radio up to his ear. I became suspicious and then every Saturday I saw him there as I sneaked past. Then the penny dropped. My suspicions were confirmed. He was a compulsive gambler.

Our relationship had to end and I was broken-hearted.

Not only had I been conned but I felt as if I had been used now that it was all over.

Even though he had helped me quit my drug problem, he had also helped himself to my money and to my body!

What made it hard for me to get over the breakup was that I realised he had taken advantage of me and also deceived me.

I was hurt as I had felt very close to him and believed in him.

However, another voice in my head told me that I had been a sucker and I now knew why his wife had left six months before I had met him.

Once again, I had been let down by a man I had trusted and cared for, and I couldn't help but wonder,

What in the Dickens was wrong with me?

Chapter 19

Choices I Had To Make

During the next three years or so, Sue got married and later on, they had two beautiful little girls, Bridie and Myfwny. Her husband, Dick, was a school teacher from Scotch College and had driven a busload of boys, who were boarders, down to Toorak College for the school dance. It was love at first sight and I was so happy for them.

Every Sunday, I visited Paul, even though it was becoming quite apparent that it was a waste of time as he did not show any signs of recognition but I still felt that I wanted to see him. He seemed as happy as he could be but the main thing was that I knew he was safe.

One Sunday afternoon, Mum came with me and we noticed a new male nurse on duty. He was from Austria and strikingly handsome with piercing blue eyes. He looked as if he belonged more on the ski slopes than in a children's institution. We seemed to be drawn to each other physically and as Mum was busy giving Paul a packet of chips, he spoke to me softly in broken English.

'Hello. My name is Kurt and I would like to personally look after Paul's safety.'

I did not understand what he was talking about at first and then he spelled it out.

'Paul is a very good-looking boy, and he could be in danger of paedophiles.'

I was shocked and horrified and could not believe it and was quick to say, 'If anything like that is going on in here, I will immediately report it to Matron Swanson.'

He cautioned me, saying, 'It hasn't yet but it would pay you to make sure that your son would never be a victim.' Then he said, very simply, 'I will guard Paul for you if you will sleep with me.'

I did not know what to think. Then I saw my lovely, innocent child, dancing around eating his chips with Mum and I knew that I had to do whatever it took to protect him. I quickly wrote down my name, address and phone number on Kurt's clipboard. Then we made a time for the day after next. I could not believe what I was doing but the thought of anything bad ever happening to Paul overshadowed any logical reasoning that I may have had normally.

I became increasingly nervous and on the day, almost called it off. However, Paul's wellbeing had to come first. Kurt was on time and I invited him in. He lost no time in finding my bedroom and taking off his clothes, and then mine. He was a fine specimen of a man with a perfectly proportioned, tanned body. Lust immediately took over and I was suitably impressed with his outstanding virility.

It was only after he left, I realised that we had not discussed anything about Paul at all. Instantly, I became suspicious. As I was under the shower, washing every trace of him off me, I wondered if this had just been an elaborate ruse to get me into bed with him. Suddenly, I felt used and totally degraded. I was determined to get to the bottom of it and if needs be, report him. However, next time I went to visit Paul, Kurt was not there. I was told that Kurt had only been there for two weeks and would never be back again, as he had just been on trial!

Apparently, he had been assessed as being unsuitable for the position.

I had been tricked. I had fallen for Kurt's story, hook, line and sinker and I went home feeling like a fool. Of course, nothing like he had insinuated would ever happen at the Cottages and I wondered how I could have been so gullible. However, I knew that I had been vulnerable and must have been a sitting shot for him. Nevertheless, I felt humiliated and was so ashamed but there was nothing I could do about it anymore, so I decided to try and forget the whole thing. Unfortunately, it was all brought back to me several days later when I was vacuuming under the bed and found a fifty-dollar note. I spent the rest of the day torturing myself as to whether the money had accidentally fallen out of Kurt's pocket or if he had left it for me as some kind of payment, or worse still, as insurance against me complaining about him. All options horrified and sickened me.

However, it turned out to be another unsolved mystery in my life as I never saw him again.

Near the end of the year, Mum decided to sell the businesses of her first two boutiques and just keep the Mount Eliza one. Then Mum and Dad sold their Mount Waverley house and bought one in Mount Eliza and I moved back home. The new house suited us better as it was bigger and had two bathrooms. Hayden had started at the Peninsula school and was doing well and loving it, and Stan was paying the school fees, which was a great help. Mum and I worked at the Mount Eliza shop and Dad had resigned from his job. He had had enough of selling earthmoving equipment and got a job as a groundsman for a car dealership and also the one-acre private garden of the manager's residence. He was a lot happier as there was no pressure on him.

One July in the school holidays, Hayden and I went to Surfers Paradise for a holiday. It was the first time we had both been on a modern jet plane and we loved it. I was so pleased to get away from Melbourne's freezing winter and we settled in well at the Chevron Hotel. As we went down the stairs to the poolside lunch area, I was aware of a man looking at me but took no notice. Then I heard him give a soft wolf whistle as he passed by and six-year-old Hayden bellowed, 'Rack off!' I was amazed, and it did my heart good to know that he was so protective of his mother, even at such a young age.

We were finding it difficult to find a vacant table for lunch and then I saw a man on his own, reading a newspaper, and I asked him if he would not mind if we shared his table with him. He smiled and said that he would be pleased if we would join him. He looked vaguely familiar to me and I suddenly realised that he was Larry Logan, a judge on a weekly Melbourne TV talent show. He said that he was in Surfers to do some big game fishing. After chatting during lunch, he invited me to have dinner with him that night and then he went off quickly to catch a big one, forgetting to book a room.

During the afternoon, Hayden and I stayed around the pool and made friends with some other mothers from Melbourne and their children. They were all ears when I told them I had met Larry Logan and that he had invited me out for dinner and they eagerly offered to mind Hayden for me instead of having a hotel babysitter.

I was so excited and chose the best outfit that I had brought with me to wear. It was a red two-piece, edged with matching crocheted lace, and the skirt was three-quarter length and tiered. I had matching red stiletto-heeled sling-back sandals, and I felt really good with my long blond hair carefully curled on the ends. I wondered what it would be like to go out with a real TV star.

After an amazing night of dining and then dancing at the Penthouse Nightclub, we got back to the hotel and Larry said that he had better check in and get a room. As he was a celebrity, the hotel had kept all his fishing gear and suitcase in a storage room while he went fishing. Apparently, he had caught a big fish that he was going to have mounted for his wall at home and it was in the freezer. It was the talk of the hotel.

I went off and got Hayden and thanked the ladies, and said that if they wanted to meet Larry, he was down at reception where he was waiting for me. They were thrilled and Larry was so charming to them. Although they were pleased for me, I could tell that at least one of them was a teeny bit jealous.

During our meal, I had found out that Larry's wife had recently left him and he was devastated. He had said that going out with me was just what he needed as I made him feel a lot better. We got on so well and I could tell that Larry and I were going to be more than just friends.

On returning to the hotel, the lady at the front desk suddenly started making grand apologies to him as there were no rooms left in the whole place because it was school holidays and she said that everywhere else would be booked out by now also. He looked worried and suddenly tired. I felt sorry for him and suggested that he share my room with Hayden and me if the hotel could arrange a spare bed.

The staff bent over backwards and carried all Larry's luggage and wheeled a trundle bed along the passage to my room. Imagine my surprise when as we passed by each of my new friends in their rooms, I caught them peeping through the cracks in their doors, gasping open-mouthed and wide-eyed at me. By now, everyone at the Chevron knew that Larry Logan was going to spend the night in my room. I thought it was funny, because at that stage, all I was trying to be was a good Samaritan. However, the next day, he got a room of his own and extended his holiday on my account, and I wondered if I was about to fall in love again! Surely not, but the way things were going, it seemed so.

Back in Melbourne, we continued to see each other for nearly two years but because he owned a business in the city, he was very busy. However, we managed to be together for a night at his home most weekends but I was starting to wonder where it was all leading to, as after all, I had a young son still at school to think about but his two children had grown up and his son still lived with him. However, I had had a bit of a wakeup call a few days before I saw him next when I read a snippet in a newspaper gossip column that said, 'Larry Logan has been spotted recently at the Silvers Nightclub living it up with well-known former radio star and actress, Shelley Goldsworthy, after his painful divorce two years ago.'

Of course, I was not amused as we had been there several times and there had been nothing written up about us. Then to cap it off, the girlfriend of Larry's son asked me if the diamond earrings she had found last week in an empty ashtray in the lounge room were mine. So I thought it was time for me to get to the crux of the matter.

Larry apologised for not telling me that he had caught up with Shelley as they were old radio friends from way back and also that he didn't mean to hurt me but then added that I was free to go out with other people if I wanted to.

Unfortunately for me, Larry did not want to ever commit himself to marriage again. He had been too badly hurt by his exwife, even though she had now remarried.

So sadly, we broke up as I had wanted more from our relationship. I had wanted to get married and live happily ever after with a husband that I loved.

Nonetheless, we still remained close friends but naturally, I was extremely hurt.

My heart was broken again but I knew that I had to find someone else – but who and where?

All I wanted was to love and to be loved.

I was still feeling sorry for myself when I heard that the psychiatric nurses in Melbourne were going to strike. This was something that had never happened before and was a very desperate plea for those dedicated people but no one was listening to their request for a well-deserved wage increase. Of course, I only had one immediate thing in mind and that was Paul and what was going to happen to him if the nurses were not there to care for him.

Then I found out that hospitals and clinics were calling on the public to help and so were the Kew Cottages. I did not hesitate and called the number in the paper. The lady explained that they were really looking for nurses and trained medical staff from other areas to help. I quickly became emotional and said that I would not rest unless I was out there helping the children in Paul's ward. So eventually she relented and put me on night duty with Vanessa, a young fully trained hospital sister, who was in her last year studying to become a psychiatric nurse. I immediately went out and bought a pair of the latest Adidas sports shoes as I thought I might have a lot of walking to do that night.

Vanessa was lovely and already knew of Paul and the children in his ward as she had spent a lot of time observing them in the course of her studies. When we arrived, the other previous volunteers had fed, bathed and put the children to bed.

I sat in the nurses' station and Vanessa showed me a file with all the children's photos. I opened it and there was Paul right on the first page, looking absolutely gorgeous and so happy as he was caught on camera jumping up into the air on a trampoline supervised by a nurse.

I proudly told Vanessa that Paul was my son and she said that she thought I must have had a special reason for wanting to be there that night with her.

The next thing she advised me was that I had better read the summary about him in his patient file and so I did.

Paul is a disturbed nine-year-old.
Normally happy and smiling but is very withdrawn – no real contact.

<u>ABSCONDER – Must be constantly supervised</u> – *finds any unlocked door.*
If he runs, it is normally down through the grounds to the Chandler Highway. Commonly runs during evening. Feeds himself, toilet trained (routine), helps in dressing. No speech, poor comprehension. Assessed as partially deaf and is also subject to infrequent temper outbursts during which he may bite himself and other children severely.
Subject to infrequent epileptic attacks.

I was shocked and Vanessa said that he had run away several times whilst she had been there but usually had been found on the grounds in a few minutes. However, she had heard that last summer he had been found on neighbours' lawns cooling off under their garden sprinklers. Apparently, the nearby residents all knew him and were quite used to ringing the Cottages if they spotted him. I was amazed and could hardly believe it. No wonder I had found him difficult to manage at home. When we went on our rounds, she showed me his bed and there he was, fast asleep like an angel with his name and the Cottage's phone number printed on his arm. It was a heart-wrenching experience for me and I finally realised that I had to let go. He didn't know me anymore and Vanessa agreed.

I had to stop dreaming the impossible dream that one day Paul would suddenly get better and be just like a normal little boy and be able to come home again. I had to come to terms with the fact that his permanent home was at the Kew Cottages and would be for the rest of his life. The other twenty-nine or so children in his ward, who had been there since birth, hardly ever had visitors and it was only now that I understood why. There is nothing more hurtful than to see your child in such a sad and hopeless situation, knowing that no matter what you do, you are unable to help them anymore.

It is the most soul-destroying thing for a parent to endure.

I thought back to the weekend before the strike and related our experience to Vanessa.

Mum and I, with Hayden, had taken Paul out in the car for an outing. We had bought Kentucky Fried Chicken beforehand, as

Paul loved it, and stopped at St James Park in Hawthorn that I remembered from childhood. We sat on a park bench with Paul in the middle between Mum and I, and we had one hand on each of his legs whilst we ate our chicken with the other free hand. Paul gulped his food down happily and we almost looked like a normal family having a picnic. I told Mum that I thought Hayden might like to sit on the old War Relic, Cannon Gun, near the War Memorial as I had years ago as a child before we left, but he had no chance of that at all. Paul was always very clever in judging the best time to break free and this was no exception. He darted across the park towards busy Burwood Road in a flash. Somehow, we managed to catch him when Mum cleverly waved another leg of chicken in the air and he momentarily stopped and grabbed it. He was so forceful that it took us all our strength to drag him back to the car. Fortunately, Hayden was able to unlock and quickly open the back car door while we pushed Paul inside. We realised then that he was too powerful for us now and we could never take him out of the Cottage's grounds again, and Vanessa nodded sympathetically.

I thanked God once more that Paul was in a safe place and well looked after. He had looked so peaceful, asleep in the dormitory. My thoughts went back to Kurt's obscene scenario and once again, I felt so ashamed at what I had done but most of all, I was still angry at what had happened, and I hated Kurt for it. The children at the Cottages were really fortunate as they were loved and protected by all the staff. There was one little girl called Mary, in Paul's ward, who had been born without arms and legs. She spent most of her time in a special kind of bouncinette and although she was cross-eyed and had a hair lip and a cleft palette, you could see that she was smiling every time one of the nurses played with her. The old Cottages were now demolished and had been replaced by very modern, comfortable new units and I was so grateful that Paul was there.

Luckily, Vanessa and I had got on very well as it had been a long night shift for us. Impulsively, I decided to ask her if she had ever run into an Austrian nurse named Kurt.

Vanessa immediately went red, nodded and swore, 'That bastard!' Then, realising we had something in common, we exchanged very interesting stories.

She, like me, had never told a soul what had happened to her and so it was a great relief to us both to know that we were not the only ones who had fallen into Kurt's carefully snared trap.

We came to the conclusion that his insatiable sexual appetite must have tripped him up somewhere down the track. Probably another gullible victim or victims had reported him after being sucked in by his good looks and clever lies.

In any case, he was gone now and it was water under the bridge, for both of us.

Chapter 20

Sunny Daze

Hayden and I were happy living in Mount Eliza with Mum and Dad. Every Sunday, Hayden and I went to church, which was in the assembly hall at his grammar school. The chaplain, Rev John Leaver, was a lovely man and so was his wife Wendy, who played the organ beautifully and taught music at the school. We became good friends, especially when I joined Wendy's church choir.

Robyn, who worked in the real estate agency near Mum's shop, became another close friend as her husband had left her with three young kids. I would often go around to her place and we would drown our sorrows about our past men with the latest invention of cask wine, or Chateau de Cardboard, as we preferred to call it.

There was also Annette, my hairdresser. She was very outgoing and had just come back from a holiday at Club Med in Tahiti on the island of Moorea. She was raving about it and suggested that I should go there and get on with my love life again as it was predominately for *singles*. So I decided to try it and saved solidly for the next few months and then set off.

At Melbourne Airport, I saw two ladies waiting to check in with Club Med folders in their hands. Sheena and Michelle were from affluent suburbs and also travelling by themselves.

We all got along well and so I had to share a bungalow with Sheena. However, she had what she thought was a serious request for me.

'If you ever see my tennis racket outside our door, then please don't come in.' Michelle and I were surprised and asked why.

'There are no locks on the bedrooms at Club Med resorts that are for *singles*. I am determined to find a rich husband here so do not want any interruptions as I will be trying them all out during the day.'

Michelle and I were amazed and turned away as we stifled a giggle.

So I spent most of the holiday outside my room but I did not care as I had met Al at the Club Med picnic. It was a great day on a deserted island and there was a relay race after we had consumed lots of Sangria with our lunch and I was in his team. Everyone found it hard to run up to a coconut on the sand for their team and run around it three times before returning to the next person. Al and I seemed to be only ones sober enough and helped win for our team. He was so much fun and after a few days, he charted a private outrigger canoe for us to see some other smaller islands. We called into a waterfront bar at one of the most beautiful secluded beaches in French Polynesia and I had my first taste of a Mai Tai cocktail. It made my day!

Al was an American and owned a casino in Las Vegas so he had shouted the holiday to three of his young trainee colleagues as a reward for their outstanding work. They were having a ball in all the water sports, tennis matches and other activities with the French GOs (gentile organisers) and so Al and I had a lot of free daytime together.

He was a perfect gentleman and there was no pressure from him to ever have sex. I was so grateful for that as I didn't want another broken heart. It seemed that we both just wanted to have platonic fun and enjoyment, which was a welcome change for me.

On the way home at the Tahiti airport, I said to the girls, 'What a shame this all has to end. During the last eight days, I have had the time of my life here.' But Sheena told us miserably, 'I hated it. There were no available rich men staying at the Club.'

Of course, I stupidly begged to differ and then she immediately wanted me to know what I meant and so I had to tell her about Al.

She was absolutely floored and became very angry. 'Why didn't you introduce him to me? He was super wealthy and was just what I was looking for. You must have known that!'

I tried to explain that I only saw Al during the day when she was busy in the bungalow. I did feel sorry for her but she had wasted so much valuable time as far as I was concerned. It was no surprise that she sulked all the way home on the plane and didn't bother speaking to us.

I felt marvellous after my wonderful holiday but soon became really bored after returning home, and so depressed with the cold Melbourne winter, that I subscribed to a series of ladies' charity luncheons at a small theatre restaurant in the city. I took Zoe, the girl who worked part-time at our shop, as she was also divorced and lonely. At the first lunch, we met the debonair host, Michael Doyle, as he mingled and flirted with all the social ladies present. He was from a wealthy family in Toorak and had a real talent for compering such events and was always in popular demand as many charities had benefited from his generous efforts.

The special guest for the day was a famous retired English car racing driver, who had had a very interesting life and we were invited to a party at his home in the penthouse of an expensive city hotel, but I could tell that Zoe was a bit apprehensive about it.

However, Michael, being the perfect host and making jokes all the time, had us in fits of laughter. I really enjoyed myself with the wine tasting and the superb food. It was the best fun I had had since my holiday in Tahiti.

As we were leaving, Michael made a special fuss of Zoe and I when he found out we had we had travelled all the way up from Mount Eliza to get there.

On the way home, Zoe said, 'I think Michael is wonderful.' We had both seen photos of him in the press before but he looked even better in real life. Then she said, 'A man like that has never given me a second look before.'

I was a bit alarmed, as I didn't want to spoil her day but I gently told her that I had seen a wedding ring on his finger. She felt disappointed but then I said in any case, there were still four more luncheons to go in the series and more new people to meet.

In four weeks, the last luncheon date had come up and I had to go earlier into town and pick up some special orders for our customers from Flinders Lane and so understandably, Zoe said she didn't really want to come.

After collecting my orders, I managed to arrive at the venue for the final luncheon on time and was amazed to see the guest car park almost empty. Michael came rushing up to me in the car park and said that the luncheon had been called off due to a fire in their kitchen late last night. I had already left Mount Eliza before he could contact me to advise of the cancellation and so he had decided to meet me in the car park with the news along with the guest speaker whom he could not reach either. People didn't have mobile phones then so Michael was doing his best to make up for our wasted trips coming into town and invited us both to have a free lunch with him at another place nearby.

Michael and I had just sat down when Blair MacLeod of MacLeod's Quality Shoes arrived, wearing a reefer jacket and a crinkled tie. Jokingly Michael had confided in me before that Blair had a favourite tie and hardly ever changed it. I laughed to myself as I was introduced to him but unfortunately, I was a bit shy and spoke mainly to Michael for the next half hour. Blair had a perfect Melbourne Grammar speaking voice and I could tell he was very intellectual. I thought that he would probably be boring and presumed that I would not be able to keep up with his conversation. However, after a glass of Michael's favourite wine, we started to find common ground. Blair had a sense of humour and loved the beach, and I found myself eagerly accepting a weekend invitation sometime to stay at *Sunny Daze*, his clifftop holiday home at Sorrento.

However, before this could happen I had to make sure it would not clash with my weekend routine. Every fortnight or so, I would drive to a McDonald's Family Restaurant and deliver Hayden to Stan for his access visit. Normally, I would go on to the Cottages after that and see Paul but now that Mum and I physically could not manage taking him out of the grounds any more, there seemed no point. He only responded to the food treats that we brought to him and still did not know us.

I explained to Stan that I wanted to scale down my visits now as I had finally come to terms with the severity of Paul's illness after being on duty during the psychiatric nurses' strike. To my amazement, he agreed to go and see him whenever he picked up Hayden. I was very relieved that Stan was now taking an interest in visiting Paul at long last. In fact, he seemed only too happy to share the burden of my ritualistic visits that had been nearly every weekend for four years. It was a load off my mind and I wondered if he had now suddenly realised that Paul's condition had not really been my fault, at all.

Sue and Dick had built a beautiful home in the hills at Emerald and so with more time to spare, I used to take Hayden to see his Auntie Sue, Uncle Dick and cousins Bridie and Myfwyny. They always had a great time together and the little girls loved their big cousin. It was also good to be able to confide in Sue and she understood perfectly why I could not bear to go and see Paul so much anymore. I was so fortunate to have such a close relationship with my kind and understanding sister. She was always busy baking whenever I popped in as they had lots of dinner parties with Dick's old college friends and their wives. They were in a lovely group of young married professionals and very happy. I always went home inspired, with some of her latest recipes.

Sue's friend Rhonda, the vicar's daughter from Glen Iris, also kept in touch and gave her all the latest news from our old Young Anglican Fellowship friends and had a bombshell to share with me. Joel had left the Anglican Church and had become a Baptist minister! Not only that, but he had married a divorcee with three children! I couldn't believe it and neither could she. In one way I was shocked but in another, I was quite pleased as it added some kind of closure to my feelings for him. It was now 1978 and it had been fourteen years since I had last seen him at Orbost but in my heart I always still had a small candle burning for him up until that moment. However, I now realised that now it had to be snuffed out for good and it was well and truly time to light a new one for someone else. Then I started to relay to Sue about Blair whom I had met through Michael Doyle, and Sue crossed her fingers for me.

The following Friday, Michael rang me at the shop and wished me a happy Christmas and good luck for my weekend with Blair as he kept a check on things when they played tennis every week at their club. He said that he had just decided to put his holiday home and his house in town on the market and he and his wife were going to move north as soon as they were sold as they wanted to retire in a warmer climate.

Then he cracked a joke and said that I wouldn't get rid of him that easily and that he could still be around for quite a while yet.

However, he hoped that Blair would be the one who would end up being the new man in my life that he knew I was seeking.

Next day, I heard from Blair and he invited me to come down on Saturday for Christmas lunch but I politely explained that traditionally, I had always had it with my family and naturally wanted to be with them and my ten-year-old son Hayden, so I would have to come down later in the afternoon. He had also suggested that I stay on until Tuesday and go home early in the morning and then I could open the shop. It was all arranged and Mum gave me her blessing and kindly offered to mind Hayden, as she usually did. I knew that all she wanted was my happiness and I loved her so much.

On the way to Sorrento, my car stereo cassette player belted out the latest Abba songs. I had just finished listening to 'Fernando' as I drove down a narrow lane off the main highway and spotted *Sunny Daze*, the name of Blair's house, on the gate. I left my car parked next to Blair's silver Mercedes and went in. It was about 3.30 p.m. and as I walked around the limestone house, I became aware that it was perched on a cliff overlooking Port Phillip Bay. I fell in love with it. It was beautiful and it even had an observation tower on the roof.

As I approached the side door, Blair came out to greet me. I wasn't ready for such an amorous kiss but it made me feel at home, considering that five people were staring out at us. I was immediately asked inside and introduced to Blair's house guests. Then I was offered a drink and invited to sit at the table for lunch. I felt very embarrassed as they had all waited for me to have lunch with them. Blair said that he wanted me to be there for their Christmas lunch and so they had decided to wait and he did not care if I didn't eat much. After a glass of wine or two, I started to feel at ease and could not get over at how friendly and polite everyone seemed to be. They were all young men from other countries, mostly from Vietnam, and some Thailand and the Philippines. Blair made it quite clear that one of his passions in life was to help support the boat people and refugees until they got their feet firmly on the ground in Australia. He was such an interesting man and so kind and generous.

The boys, as he referred to them, cleared the table and washed up whilst Blair took me on a tour of inspection of his property. He asked me if I had some rubber thongs as my platform sole shoes were not suitable for the beach. I said that I did have some in my overnight bag but he suggested that I might like to borrow some of his spare ones to save me going into my room. I presumed that the thongs would be samples from his shoe factory but I was wrong. He pointed to a plastic bucket on the veranda that had thongs of all sizes and colours but none matching. Blair said that he and the boys often found single thongs washed up on the beach and they would be added to the collection in the box for everyone to use. What a joke! I had to contain myself from laughing out loud. He was such an intriguing man. As I did not like the thought of wearing someone else's second-hand thongs, I opted to go and get mine while he waited.

When I came back, I saw him standing by the flag pole, looking out to sea, and he was wearing a pair of blue speedos and one green thong and one blue one. He smiled and took my arm and we went down the private cliff path to the beach. It was like something out of a movie and I was enthralled. It was years since I had been to Sorrento but it felt so familiar as the sand was the same as I had remembered at Rosebud. We walked along Blair's private little jetty, saw his motorboat tied up and decided to go fishing one day soon. I was in my element as we continued walking hand-in-hand up to Point King. I felt so proud to be by his side. Blair was tall and slim and his blonde curls shone like gold in the late afternoon sun. He had an air of authority about him and really looked the part as he was already sporting a sun tan. He seemed to have endless energy and I found it difficult to keep up with him, so I stopped several times and asked him who lived in the various mansions that we were passing. It was fascinating to know the history of all the families that had handed down their houses from one generation to another.

My afternoon had been completely different to what I had expected, and I found myself respecting and admiring Blair at every turn. He was so concerned about all the boys and kept encouraging them about studying and or finding work in the New Year. I gathered that they were living with him temporarily and I could tell that they were all grateful that Blair had taken them in. I was amused as they all seemed to have a quirky sense of humour that I found quite sweet. However, the thing that impressed me the most was that they all adored Blair.

Later on after dinner, I asked Blair about his family. He said that his mother was still alive and he had a married sister, Heather. Then he suddenly looked sad and said that his twin daughters, Lexie and Justine, had grown up and were celebrating Christmas with his ex-wife. I immediately felt that I had touched a raw nerve and that it wasn't any of my business and maybe I had overstepped the mark. I felt terrible, as I had not meant to pry. However, he said that the girls would be calling in to see him during January as he would be there for the whole month. I was so pleased to hear that and I hoped that I would have the opportunity to meet them.

After a long day, I retired to the girls' room, as it was called. It was a pink bedroom with pink floral bedspreads on single beds and very girly. I had just showered and changed into a pretty nightie when I heard a gentle knock on the door.

I invited Blair inside and it wasn't long before I realised that at last, I had found a ten-out-of-ten man, for me.

He was perfect!

Chapter 21

Such Is Life

I spent every weekend in January with Blair at *Sunny Daze* including New Year's Eve and then up at his riverside house in town most weekends for the next year. I knew that I was in love with him and I believed that he was with me. It was now 1979; I was thirty-six and Blair was fifty-one but I never even thought about the age difference. After all, I idolised Paul Newman and he was about the same age as Blair.

It was only when my mother questioned me a bit further about Blair that she confirmed her suspicions and threw a spanner in the works. Blair had been married to one of her cousins and the whole family had been mystified when she had divorced him, considering that they had two children and that that branch of the family had always frowned on divorce. I still didn't let it worry me, as there were always two sides to a story. I just wanted to keep on enjoying my happiness and could not bear to think of it ever ending. Anyway, at least Michael was happy for me, now that I had found my ten out of ten.

It wasn't long before Christmas came around again and this time Blair had sold the runabout boat that we had all crowded into before and had bought a trailer sailer, which he called *Moon Shadow*. We had a memorable Boxing Day aboard, watching the start of the Portsea to Devonport Yacht Race. I was packing a picnic but needed cranberry sauce for the cold turkey sandwiches. One of the boys drove to the shops to get some for me but it held us up and when we got out on the water, it was impossible for us to get a good view. There were boats everywhere. Then someone said that there was a spot a bit further out that for some unknown reason, everyone had left clear. It was a perfect vantage point and we quickly made for it. We were enjoying our champagne and gourmet sandwiches when a police boat came by and shouted through a megaphone to leave the spot immediately. We were annoyed and Blair took his time on purpose as the race was about to start. Just then, we heard a deafening sound and to our horror, we looked around and saw a passenger liner coming straight for us. Fortunately, we managed to get out of the shipping lane in the nick of time. It was such an exciting day and one that we would never forget.

Another weekend, we decided to go surfing at the back beach. It was crowded, of course, but I need not have worried. We climbed down the steep cliff to the beach, with the boys carrying our towels, my beach bag, a rug and the picnic basket. We really must have stood out in those days and I could see all the snooty Portsea Push, as they were known, whispering to each other as our Asian entourage went by. When we found a spot of sand, it was incredible the way people moved away but this only made more room for us. The boys dug comfortable hollows for Blair and me to lie in and then spread out our towels over them like staff at a resort. We were the centre of attention and I loved it. How boring everyone else was. I was having the time of my life and felt that I could do anything, when I was with Blair and his charges. They had all done so well in their endeavours during the year and we also had some new ones staying with us. I likened Blair to a Pied Piper as he led us up to the car when we left the beach, and I didn't care what the Portsea snobs thought.

It was the end of January and I had enjoyed yet another summer of weekends at *Sunny Daze* and was driving back to Mount Eliza, listening to my favourite Abba tape as they sang, 'Money, money, money, must be funny, in a rich man's world.'

I could not have agreed more. It was obvious that Blair came from a prosperous family and was continuing to carry on the success of his family's footwear empire but he never flaunted his wealth. He was so unpretentious and lived almost frugally. Even his Mercedes was an old cast-off from his father. Whenever he or the boys needed new clothes or shoes, they would do the rounds of his favourite second-hand shops. I was quite surprised at first, as being in the rag trade, I always had new clothes every season but I soon got used to Blair's endearing characteristics. After all, the number of people he had helped settle in Australia was quite staggering.

On Australia Day, he had a reunion of some of the old boys he had helped with their wives and children, who had recently arrived legally from overseas and we had a seafood barbecue to celebrate and afterwards enjoyed a lively game of cricket on the beach. It never ceased to amaze me how Blair could make a meagre catch of flathead feed so many people. It was almost like the feeding of the five thousand but instead of the loaves, he served mountains of rice with salad. As everyone posed for a photo on the top of the cliff, I thought to myself that it looked like the League of Nations. That was, of course, why I loved Blair so much. He loved everyone, black, white or brindle. He loved people for who they were and not what they had. He was not materialistic and was completely unconventional. I found myself becoming very like him in a lot of ways as I started to hate the mundane way of life. I was sad that the holidays had ended as I had come to look upon *Sunny Daze* as part of my life. We had a huge clean-up as February was the month of the year when Blair's mother had the use of the house and it would be filled with her friends. It was hard for me to believe that other people also occupied the house as apart from Blair's daughters who had dropped in on several occasions, I had never seen his mother.

I continued to pop up to town for weekends to see Blair at his South Yarra home and because I was so happy, I started feeling guilty about Paul. Unfortunately, the older Paul got, the more apparent it became that he would never be normal. I became so distressed after visiting him during Easter that I decided not to see him again.

Then, out of the blue, I received a call from Michael who said that he knew Blair and I were having a lovely time as he had been receiving glowing reports from Blair at their tennis club. He said that he was so glad but the reason for the call was to say goodbye as he was leaving for Queensland in a few weeks. I was sorry that he was going but nevertheless pleased for him as he had decided that it was really what he wanted to do, as he had had enough of running his vineyards and had sold them at a very good price. I thought that it would be a good idea if Blair and I invited him to lunch before he went, and so I said that I would try to arrange it as soon as I could.

The year was starting to get colder and when I saw Blair the following weekend, he said that he was looking forward to his annual business trip away to the Philippines in the tropics. He joked that it was boiling hot there but every time he came back, he always arrived home with a bad cold. We agreed it was a shame that we would have to cancel Michael's farewell lunch but business was business. However, I was a bit miffed. After all, I thought that it was the least we could have done, as if it had not been for Michael, Blair and I would have never met each other.

When Blair departed for his overseas trip, I felt so alone and at a loose end. I tried to make light of it to myself as I knew it would not be forever but a whole month to wait to see him again seemed like a whole lifetime to me.

Then at last, one day, I received a letter from Blair and could not wait to tear it open. It was quite a long letter and I felt so excited that he had taken so much time in putting pen to paper. My joyful anticipation suddenly turned to dismay and disbelief. I was dumbfounded. I wanted to scream. I wanted to cry but nothing came out. I was fearful and ran to my room, collapsing on my bed. The sentence below crushed me.

'I am very sorry, but I have decided to marry a pen friend, Yasmin (Min), who is a servant girl from the Island of Cebu and I am bringing her back with me at the end of the month.'

I had never heard of this girl before and doubted very much if he loved her. Why had he not told me before this? It was all very peculiar and I did not know where to turn. I decided to have a brandy to settle me down and then I had the courage to telephone Blair's mother. She and I had never met but she seemed to know who I was and was absolutely appalled when I told her the contents of her son's letter. She said that she would certainly put a stop to such a marriage and would disinherit Blair if he went against her wishes. She was very nice and I apologised for causing her so much worry but she ended up thanking me.

The next day, I begged Michael to come down and see me at the shop. Mum and I were both working that day and she was so upset at the whole thing but of course did not blame Michael. She said that in the back of her mind, she had not felt comfortable about my relationship with Blair because of her cousin's experience but had not interfered as she had only wanted me to be happy. Michael nearly died when he read the letter and was panic-stricken. He put his arms around me, offering his commiserations. He said that he was amazed that this had happened and, like me, could not understand why. To make matters worse, he said that he was leaving Victoria the next day and would not be able to mediate for me.

As he drove away, I felt so alone.

Then suddenly, I wondered if Blair's boys had a clue. I had to find out!

I had nothing to lose as I had already lost my heart and my soul.

After work, I broke all the speed limits up to South Yarra. I noticed Blair's front door wide open and so I walked right in. I was quickly welcomed as the boys were pleased to see me. It felt a bit strange to be there without Blair in the house but I was made to feel at home and was shown a chair without study books on it. They all wanted me to stay for dinner but unfortunately, what I wanted to know could not wait any longer. I told them that I had received a letter from Blair and they were all ears. I had circled the paragraph that I wanted them to hear and I read it out to them. There were cries of disbelief and I could tell that they were as puzzled as I was. Then, I showed them the letter and let them read the relevant part themselves. They were obviously upset and all looked uncomfortable. Then I asked them if there was something they could tell me about Blair that I did not know. I had to try and piece this thing together and so again I implored them to tell me anything at all that may help us to understand what was going on.

All at once, I could tell that they did know something but were deliberately holding back. They seemed to be very guarded and seemed to be trying to protect me. I burst into tears and told them that I loved Blair and that I always would, no matter what happened and that all I wanted to know was to why he had chosen to marry this little servant girl, Min, instead of me. I could tell that they did not really know either but I was certain that they knew something that they weren't telling me. Then I decided to ask them if they thought that Blair loved me or had ever loved me. They all said that they knew he loved me more than any other woman as he had told them. Then, all of a sudden, the newest and youngest boy, Wayan, from Bali, who had become a student at Melbourne High School, let the cat out of the bag. I had bought him a second-hand uniform for school and he was so pleased with it that he had worn it on weekends as well and I think that I may have been a kind of mother figure to him.

He came up to me and said in a gentle voice, *'Do you know that Blair is bisexual?'*

The poor boy was momentarily ostracised by the others as they were all visibly upset. Then Kim, the longest-standing member of the household, said gently that Blair loved me but he loved them, as well. They were all in shock about his intentions with Min and now that I had found out Blair's secret, they were really worried as they were very loyal and grateful people.

When we had all calmed down, I thanked them for being honest and said that I would not tell Blair of our conversation as naturally, they would speak to him first when he came home with Min and would tell them of his future plans. I could see no point at this stage in getting them involved in my relationship with Blair. I blew a kiss to them all as I went to go out the door and told them that I would never betray them and that as far as I was concerned, I would still love Blair. Then I told them I knew that Blair's mother would never allow the marriage to take place and they cheered, and they all blew kisses back to me.

As I drove home, I tried to fathom it all out. If it was true that Blair was bisexual, then why hadn't he told me? And why was he bringing a girl back from the Philippines to Australia to marry? If he wanted to get married, then why wasn't he going to marry me? I knew that he loved me. Maybe he didn't want to hurt me. But this had hurt me more, hearing of his marriage plans with another woman in a letter. I knew that he was still upset after his first marriage break up but that was years ago. I supposed that he had already had one Australian wife who was not willing to share him with anyone else, let alone young men! And so I imagined that he wouldn't want that to happen again. Maybe he felt the Filipino girl would not mind but that I would!

I felt sorry for everyone. Obviously, Blair could not help the way he was made. That was the reason that I was attracted to him. He loved everyone! Unfortunately, for me, I realised that he would never be able to give up his bisexuality and although I didn't want to face up to it, I had to come to terms with it. I had to admit that this kind of relationship was not really what I had hoped for or remotely had envisaged. I realised that if all of this was true, then Blair was right. In his letter, he had said that it never would have worked out with us. I was so disappointed and I felt as if a rug had been pulled out from underneath me.

When I arrived home, Mum was waiting for me. We had a quiet talk and she did not seem to be at all surprised. Apparently, she had been on the phone to Auntie Beth and had found out the real reason for their cousin's divorce. Mum had been right in her suspicion of Blair but I did not want to discuss it anymore and went to bed completely worn out.

All night, I tossed and turned and came to the conclusion that Blair had never wanted to hurt me and so I decided I would keep the peace and make friends with Min and see what happened next. I was sure that the marriage would not go ahead, but then I wondered what the poor girl would do in a strange country, possibly not speaking much English. It was all such a mess and I couldn't wait for Blair to come home and sort it all out.

For the next weeks, I found it difficult to eat or sleep and be interested in anything. Then one morning, Blair phoned and said he was back in Australia and invited me down to Sorrento for the weekend. It took me by surprise but I said that I thought it best if I just came down only for the afternoon on Saturday. Then I told him I had received his letter and I asked him about Min. He said that as she of course would be there with him and he hoped I would like her. Then he asked me if I had telephoned his mother. I replied truthfully that I had and he said calmly that we would talk further on Saturday, face to face.

Saturday arrived at long last. The journey to *Sunny Daze* was unpleasant to say the least. Even playing Abba did not help. I felt like an intruder and had butterflies in my stomach as I parked the car. Blair came out to meet me and kissed me as usual. The boys were there and then I saw a tiny slip of a girl with long black hair and shiny black eyes staring at me timidly. I offered the hand of friendship and I could see that she was very relieved. We went inside and I gave her a parcel of new woollen jumpers and warm clothes as I had predicted she would only possess light clothing and it was winter here. Blair had given her a jumper of his to wear but it was huge and unattractive. She was overjoyed to receive my gifts and everyone, including the boys, were happy to see that I bore no grudge. How could I? Min was totally innocent and I felt sorry for her. In fact, I felt sorry for us all and I was quite relieved that I had made it clear that I wasn't going to stay for the night. I could not have coped if there had been a knock on my bedroom door.

After afternoon tea, when alone in the garden, Blair told me that he was not going to marry Min as his mother had threatened to disinherit him. I laughed to myself and asked him straight out if he really loved her. He immediately admitted that he didn't and so I asked him why he didn't want to marry me. He looked broken-hearted and said that he could not bear another marriage break-up like his first one and that it would not be fair on me, or him. In other words, it would never work out.

I told him that I found out that he was bisexual and I really wanted to know why he had never told me. He said that he had tried many times but could not bear to tell me. We embraced and I said that I would always love him in any case, and he said that he would love me forever. We sincerely believed each other and shared a goodbye kiss, marking the end of our relationship.

As we walked back to the house, I mentioned that I had booked a holiday to Club Med, leaving the next day for Malaysia and Borneo. The side trip to Sarawak was going to take my mind off everything as I was going to visit the longhouses in the jungle inhabited by the Ibans, whose ancestors had been head-hunters. Blair was fascinated and said he wished he was coming too but realised that anything like that was now out of the question. Before I left, I asked about Min's future and he said that she wanted to stay in Australia, even though he had offered to pay her fare back to Cebu. He thought that he would have no trouble finding her a live-in domestic job with a nice, respectable family.

We could not resist one last kiss and I promised to send him a postcard. It was so sad.

I put my head in the doorway and said goodbye to the boys and Min came rushing out, wearing one of my jumpers and a pair of matching track pants. I thought that the pale blue colour really suited her. I hugged her and wished her all the best and then took one last look at the beautiful old house and the view from the cliff over the bay. I knew things would never be the same again.

Then, totally dejected, I left *Sunny Daze* possibly for the last time.

I continued to feel miserable driving home but as everything had now been resolved, my visit there had ended up on a positive note.

After all, we were still going to be best friends for the rest of our lives!

When I arrived home, Mum was relieved that I had come to some kind of amicable farewell arrangement and was glad that I was taking off on a holiday. She was not the only one. I telephoned Sue and brought her up to date on everything that had happened and she said that I really needed to get away. I sent my love to Dick and the girls and said that I would come home in three weeks or so with presents from a stopover in Singapore. I started to get excited and found myself packing suitable summer clothes and my bikini.

It was going to be perfect therapy as I had always hated Melbourne's freezing winter.

Chapter 22

A Turning Point

Next day, I woke up with a new focus and later that afternoon, I found myself sitting in economy class on a Malaysian Airlines aircraft but feeling as if I was having a first-class time. The air hostesses all looked so beautiful in their orange, gold and black silk uniforms. They soon found out that I liked the free champagne and offered it to me endlessly until I felt that I had a sufficient amount and wanted to have a nap before dinner. As I was drifting off to sleep, I examined my life. I felt excited about the trip and relaxed with the help of the alcohol, but I wondered how many other ladies in their thirties had had a divorce, had to place their Profoundly Autistic child in an institution and were trying to get over their immense love of a bisexual boyfriend!

I certainly did not set out to put myself in such incredible circumstances.

Just before I dozed off completely, I wondered what lay in store for me as I knew I could never forget my beautiful Blair but of course, I realised that we would always have a special bond even though our sexual life was over, but it was going to be very difficult for me.

Next morning, I went on a quick conducted tour of Kuala Lumpur and inspected a temple but it did nothing for me. I could not wait to catch the small plane to Kuantan late in the afternoon as I was dying to start my holiday at Club Med, Cherating. However, the Kuala Lumpur airport in 1980 was a culture shock for Westerners like me. I was busting to go to the ladies' before boarding the small plane and imagine my disgust upon entering it, when I had to walk on wet concrete covered in urine to get to a hole in the floor that had no proper sewerage. I nearly threw up at the sight and stench and rushed out when I had finished as fast as I could. I had never experienced anything like that before and couldn't believe that there were no separate cubicles and no privacy whatsoever. The lack of hygiene appalled me and made me long for a hot shower with plenty of soap as I felt contaminated. I was so glad that I had carried tissues and grateful that I had been vaccinated against all the horrible diseases we did not have in Australia as I had really felt at risk.

After a long boring trip on a minibus from the small Kuantan airport, we arrived at the Club at about 10.00 pm. I was so tired but got my second wind the minute we got to the gate. The security guards smiled at us and we drove in. We were told by the driver that the whole Club Med village had to be guarded day and night as there were *pirates* in the South China Sea. It sounded very much like a Peter Pan story but it was true. The other passengers on the Club Med bus were all also excited as we alighted and immediately got into the spirit of things. We were on holidays and there was a special team waiting for us. The music was playing an upbeat latest hit and we were given tropical floral leis to wear. It was such a warm welcome and when we saw where we were being led, it was as if we were entering a wooden palace in another world. Though it was late at night, it was all lit up like a circus and there were people swimming in a gigantic pool and sipping drinks in and out of the water. The whole place seemed abuzz and we could hear music from a disco somewhere, the drums thumping. It was wonderful. We were seated at a table overlooking the pool and given a welcome drink and a snack. I immediately felt at home as it was the same format as Club Med Moorea in Tahiti, only this was in the middle of the Malaysian jungle. It was just what I needed and I soon forgot all about my worries at home.

It was after midnight when I headed for bed. A handsome Frenchman named Pierre showed me to my room and said that he would look out for me if I wished to learn yoga or archery as he was the chief instructor for both.

I fell into bed very tired and, as this club had recently just opened, I was the first guest to sleep in my room. It smelt very new and I felt so comfortable as if a tremendous weight had been lifted from my shoulders. Everyone in the whole place was having fun and pleased to see me. I suddenly felt my self-esteem rising as I realised I had made the right decision. Why shouldn't I enjoy myself? I deserved a happy holiday and I was going to have it!

I woke up to brilliant sunshine and warm air. How I loved it. As I stepped out the door, I was enchanted to see the lush green jungle backdrop and colourful tropical flowers everywhere. My favourite was frangipani, and I picked one and put it behind my left ear, which I had learnt in Tahiti that meant that *I was available*.

No sooner had I reached the dining room when Pierre, who was on host duty, greeted me in French and I found myself replying,

'Bonjour,' in my limited school French accent. After breakfast, I had my first archery lesson with him. Pierre was the best-looking GO in the village and I felt really exhilarated.

Afterwards, I reported to reception when I discovered a note under my door. The organisers of the tour to Borneo wanted to see me so I reported to reception immediately. They were checking up on the fitness of everyone who wanted to take the side excursion. They asked me in their French accent if I was 'sportive', which I took to mean active and good at sport. I had to tell them that I only enjoyed swimming but had not done any for six months. They pointed out that on the brochure it had said that this trip was suitable for the fit and adventurous only. I was given a list of their preferred more vigorous sports to take up and then I was delighted to see that sailing was included. I had always wanted to learn to sail and so here was my chance. However, before I left, they warned me that they would be keeping a watchful eye on me and if I did not reach their standard of physical fitness, I would have to forfeit the excursion. I was a bit put out, to say the least, as I had paid for the trip in advance but I soon realised that it probably was for my own good.

Joy, my roommate from Perth, was a lovely new friend and about to turn forty. We ended up having a great party for her because her birthday was on Bastille Day, when the whole village, being French, went into party mode and celebrated for twenty-four hours non-stop.

Also, every night there was live entertainment in their theatre and all talented staff members suddenly became professional singers, dancers and actors. I used to look forward to the show every night, particularly because Pierre had a leading role as Tarzan wearing only a leopard skin loin cloth on his tanned supple physique. He performed so well, swinging and sliding down from great heights on ropes, much to gasps of wonder from the audience, to rescue Jane, who was one of the staff.

Joy and I were often called up on stage to participate in skits and then one night, we were asked if either of us could sing. My rendition of 'The Way We Were' was very well received and so from then on, I was a regular every night. I was in my element with costumes galore to choose from and a musical director and producer to help me with my songs. I was having the best holiday of my life and I still had the side trip to go.

I had come alive but all of a sudden, after two wonderful weeks, it was my last night at the Club. I had certainly achieved so much and was on a natural high, even though Joy had left the day before. After the show, Pierre asked me if he could say goodbye to me privately. I knew what he meant and I had been thinking about it for quite a while. Maybe it would help me get Blair out of my mind and it would not hurt him anyway, so I gave in and said yes. I had heard that Frenchmen were excellent lovers and I wasn't disappointed.

Next morning, all available staff and a lot of the guests lined up to say goodbye to us as there were about twenty-five people leaving and seven of those were coming with me to Sarawak. I kissed Pierre goodbye and he asked me to print my name and address for him. Having no paper, I dashed to reception to get some and as I was turning to leave, Mimi handed me a postcard that had just come in from the mail on our bus. I was surprised and grabbed it in a hurry and stuffed it into my bag. As I handed my details to Pierre, I saw tears in his eyes and I felt guilty as I could tell that he was going to miss me more than I him.

Just then, the farewell music started blaring and our coach drove off, and then I was the one who found it hard not to cry; not just for Pierre but for everyone and everything that had made my holiday so special.

I had spent every day walking a kilometre to and from the sailing shack, and then also helping to carry a laser yacht across hot sand into the water and then back again after the lesson. At the end of ten days, I could sail single-handed and re-float the vessel after capsizing.

Wow! I had qualified for my proficiency certificate and was fitter than I had ever been.

The bus trip back to the Kuantan seemed so much shorter this time because it was daylight and I was amongst friends. The people going on the excursion were two couples in their late forties from Canberra who were used to snow skiing, two French ladies who did not speak English and our tour guide, Andre. We all flew back to Kuala Lumpur, said goodbye to our other new-found friends going home and then caught our connecting flight to Kuching, the capital of Sarawak in Borneo.

We all enjoyed a lovely dinner in Kuching at our hotel, the Holiday Inn. I was fitter now than I had ever been and ready to face the Sarawak Jungle the next day.

Just before I went to sleep, I remembered the postcard in my bag that I received as I was leaving the Club. It was from Michael, wishing me a happy holiday and 'not to do anything that he wouldn't do!' Laughingly, I put it away safely as I knew I would never see him again.

It was a very exciting and challenging side trip excursion. After three hours in four-wheel drive vehicles, we at last reached the Skrang River in the second division of Sarawak and were immediately transferred with the help of some local guides who were now part of our tour group into dugout canoes. I had never seen a dugout canoe before, which was a hollowed-out tree trunk. They were very solid and had thin wooden seats and were not very comfortable. Thank goodness I had bought a small blow-up pillow in Kuching which I also used as a cushion.

The whole round trip took five days and the further we went into the jungle, the more primitive it became. The first night was spent in a guest longhouse that had been adapted for Westerners with two water closet toilets, two wash basins and wooden bunks with thin mattresses. It had steps up into the house, which was on wooden stilts and two metres above the ground. As we went inside, we were greeted by a friendly local group of Ibans but we could not help looking above us and seeing human skulls hanging above the entrance. Andre assured us that they were well over eighty years old and that head-hunting was now obsolete.

The next few days, as our canoes took us further into the jungle, Andre said that we had to realise that the people we were to meet were not used to seeing white people. It was not a problem for me as I got on well with them. Every night was the same, wherever we went. After the evening meal with black tea, some of the Iban men put on a musical show of gong-playing and in return, we gave them presents, which consisted of cigarettes for the men and lollies for the women and children. They were lovely people.

However, it was quite a feat to climb up about three metres

into the original longhouses as they were built up on lengthy bamboo stilts and the way up was only by a long-notched log with a flimsy hand rail. I was always glad to get in safely but the floor was unstable and rocked as it was made of bamboo cross strips for ventilation. It was very frightening at first as there was such a life-threatening drop below.

I was quite panic-stricken one night as I had to negotiate the dangerous exit at two o'clock in the morning as nature had called and would not wait. I found it extremely difficult to hold a torch and climb down the log into the darkness and land safely on the ground. The next part was equally hard as I searched for spot to go for a twinkle. I lifted up my sarong and squatted down. Mid-stream, I heard all the weird jungle sounds and imagined the tethered wild pigs kept under the house to eat food scraps coming for me. It was only after I made it safely back inside that I discovered that the only things that had attacked me were mosquitoes and I was bitten all over my bottom where I had neglected to apply my insect repellent.

The last day was at the furthest longhouse and we had to climb a mountain. We were warned that it would be difficult but I decided to try it. We had to leave at first light in the morning to avoid the hot midday sun. Remarkably, everyone wanted to come but it wasn't very long before Margaret and June from Canberra had to turn back. It was tough-going and we had to use the roots of trees as steps to climb up the steepest parts. We each carried a bamboo pole as a walking stick to help fend off anything nasty in the undergrowth, which in some places was over our heads. Almost at the top of the mountain, the track reached a narrow plateau of land with a deep valley far below without a bridge to cross it. My heart sank as I hated heights and wondered how I was going to negotiate it. I decided that the best thing to do was to look straight ahead, and not down, to cross safely. The guide suggested that I carry the pole tightly with two hands horizontally in a monkey grip at arm's length pointing at him as he was safely on the other side ready to catch me. I was absolutely terrified but the strategy worked and I felt so relieved and grateful to be alive afterwards. But I had done it!

At long last, we reached our final destination and the people we came to see were extremely shy. However, these Ibans turned out to be most hospitable and offered us hot black tea.

At first, though, the men were quite suspicious of me, seeing I was a white lady with long blond hair, and the women thought that I looked funny and laughed at me. The dear little children ran away and hid until they thought it was safe to come out, coincidentally, when Andre brought out the lollies. We were lying down resting on the floor when one by one, some of the little girls they came up to me and tried to rub the pink nail polish off my toe nails. They were so sweet and I was enchanted with them. An hour later, I felt quite sad having to leave my new little friends but we had to set off again in order to get back before dark.

After a long gruelling climb down and facing the leap of faith again, we arrived back safely at the longhouse, in time for the usual dinner of pineapple, watermelon, hard-boiled eggs and baked beans washed down by black tea. Then, exhausted, we fell asleep on the floor, as we had an early start the next day.

Our canoes took us back through the beautiful lush tropical jungle and quiet waters and then all of a sudden, we were in treacherous rapids. We all had to hang on tight with all our strength until we made it through safely.

After the last night at the guest longhouse, it was back to the hotel where things got back to normal quickly with a delightful dinner and copious glasses of wine.

I had had the most wonderful time of my life!

The next morning, we had our last breakfast together at the Holiday Inn and all gutsed ourselves on Western food like we had the night before. We made return visits to the hot and cold buffet, carefully avoiding pineapple, watermelon, boiled eggs and baked beans, which had been our staple diet in the jungle. It was so luxurious to have a choice of tea or coffee with milk as we had not had any milk for days in the jungle.

Next stop was the Kuching airport and we were on our way to Singapore. I was so excited and did not want this marvellous holiday to end. As I sipped my free champagne on the plane, I reflected upon the beautiful Iban people. They had been so kind opening their homes to us, even though we had had to sleep on the floor in a long line with the rest of them. It was their way of life and they had shared everything that they had with us.

It had been a tremendous eye-opener as materially, they all had very little but they were the happiest people I had ever met. I really hoped that the Western world would not spoil it all by logging and ruining their natural habitat. So many of the wild animals would be in danger of extinction and this made me very concerned.

Before we knew it, we had landed at Singapore and enjoyed shopping for gifts and our farewell dinner with Andre and then the highlight of our night: a visit to Bugis Street. The transvestites were absolutely beautiful and it was hard to believe that they were really men but of course, I wasn't surprised at anything anymore.

The following day, I was suddenly on the plane heading home. I settled back with my glass of champagne and thought how lucky I had been to have had such an amazing time. I had learnt a lot and had achieved so much on my own. I felt stronger than I had ever been before, both physically and mentally and having that memorable night with Pierre had helped me so much.

I knew that when I stepped off the plane into the freezing Melbourne winter, I could now do anything!

I had made a momentous decision. Hayden and I were going to move away at the end of the year when he finished his school year if he agreed, and start a new life in sunny Queensland!

CHAPTER 23

On The Move

Time flew and at last it was February of 1981. We arrived at Hervey Bay in Queensland and managed to find a small furnished holiday cottage to rent temporarily from week to week.

The main problem was that there was no work for me there. I was finding it difficult to manage on a single mother's pension and then my station wagon blew up. It cost a mint to fix because it was a Volvo and they had to order parts, so we had some very lean weeks. I was thinking of moving to the Sunshine Coast as Mum kept in touch with Aimee, an old family friend who used to work in one of her shops, and she apparently loved living there, so I gave notice to the real estate agency.

However, before we could leave, the locals started battening down for a cyclone. What an experience! We had never been in a cyclone before and were absolutely terrified. Everything had to be brought inside that was not fixed and we had to tape up all the windows. Then the power went off and the pitch-black night seemed endless as we huddled together on my double bed with a torch and a transistor radio. The winds were so powerful that the whole house seemed to shake. Cyclone Cliff had hit neighbouring Fraser Island, which saved us from bearing the full brunt of it but I had had enough of this place.

Next day when we were leaving, there was flooding, parts of roofs blown off, uprooted trees and debris everywhere, making it hard for us to find a way out onto the main highway.

On the Sunshine Coast, renting a house was difficult as the rents were much higher than in Hervey Bay but luckily, we ended up finding a near-new modern three-bedroom townhouse at Coolum Beach. I couldn't wait to see the beach and so upon our arrival, we ran down and had our first swim.

We settled in well and I immediately set up a housework agency from home.

I had ladies converge on the unit to be interviewed for work, and soon started to reap the rewards. Of course, the population was nothing like Melbourne, but my little business helped keep the wolf away from the door and didn't interfere with my pension.

Then one afternoon, I was in a local supermarket and absorbed in trying to get the best value for my money when I heard a familiar voice behind me. I turned around and then to my amazement, there was Michael! I couldn't believe it! Then we both found out that we lived only suburbs away. How incredible! I was so pleased to see him and invited him around the next day to catch up for morning tea.

When Michael arrived at my place the next day, he was intrigued to see me hard at work, answering non-stop phone calls from clients of my Suncoast Domestic Services and watching me match the jobs with the workers I had on my books. I had a desk in the lounge room and there were cards spread all over the dining room table.

During coffee and cake, I thanked him for his card, which I had received at Cherating and he was fascinated as I relayed my adventures. Then he asked me if I had heard from Blair and I said that we only exchanged Christmas cards from now on and I was hoping to meet someone new through my gourmet circle club that I was starting soon.

Then Michael almost begged me to let him help me run it as he could help interview prospective members for me. He said that he was finding retired life boring and as a result, he was driving his wife mad as he had nothing to do, and so of course, I said yes.

We discussed the format of the club and Michael's ideas were very good, particularly with getting free publicity from the press. Before I knew it, he had contacted the social editor of the local paper and she had given him an interview over the phone and arranged for a photographer to take our photos. I was really impressed.

After he left, I went out to the mailbox and saw that Mum had written me a letter and forwarded on a late Valentine's Day card from Pierre which made me smile. However, my happiness soon turned to shock, horror and sadness as I read that she had developed breast cancer and was about to have her right breast removed.

The thought of my beautiful mother being disfigured for life was so abhorrent to me, but then the thought of her being in danger of losing her life was even worse. I was so upset and I telephoned her immediately. I asked her if there was anything I could do but all she wanted were my prayers. The operation was due the next day and I wished her all the best and told her that I loved her more than anything. It had been so sudden and I felt guilty that I was not by her side in her time of need as she had always been for me.

Dad rang the next day and said that Mum had come through the operation satisfactorily but she would still have to have radiotherapy treatment. He seemed to be holding up well and had been talking to Sue, who sent her love. Then he went on to say that he wanted Mum to retire. It seemed like a good idea to me as she had been supporting our family for years.

Secretly, I hoped that they would come up to Queensland and live near us as we really missed them. However, I decided to save my thoughts on that until I knew that Mum was back on her feet and able to consider such a big decision.

Two weeks later, I was next in hospital as my periods had become so heavy and lasted for nearly two weeks each month, which I absolutely hated. The gynaecologist said that I had fibroids and that I needed a partial hysterectomy, which meant that my uterus would have to be removed. After careful consideration, I opted for a vaginal operation so as not to leave a scar on my tummy. Michael drove me to the hospital and Aimee, who was living at Peregian Beach, minded Hayden for me for a few nights.

After the operation, it was excruciatingly painful and as it had been performed through the vagina, the surgeon had decided to tighten everything up down there as after having two babies, my body had sagged. I felt like I was sitting astride, naked, on a barbed wire fence.

Next day, Michael came and picked me up and drove me home but although the pain had diminished, I felt that something was not quite right.

I rang the surgery in desperation and had to make an appointment with a locum doctor as mine was on holidays. He was very clinical and told me that all I needed was to have intercourse three times a week with my husband and then the scar tissue would not have a chance to knit together as that was the problem. After explaining that I was divorced, he lent me a cold, hard, stainless-steel specula to insert and return at the next consultation. *Yuck!*

Marcus was nice a member of the gourmet circle and a pharmacist and understood what I was going through. He kindly offered his personal service to me for a week. However, after I healed, he still wanted to continue; that is, until Bianca, an attractive kindergarten teacher from Sydney, joined the gourmet circle and I was more than happy to introduce her to him as I had really wanted to end it.

As months went by, it was quite apparent that the gourmet club was a great success and Michael still remained determined to be part of it, even though he had accepted a part-time position of centre manager at Sugar Town Shopping Centre in Maroochydore from Joseph Abrahams, one of the owners that he knew from Melbourne, and I was pleased for him.

Meanwhile, Mum's health continued to improve and with her determined will, she surprised us all by recuperating earlier than anyone expected, even though the radiotherapy had really taken its toll on her. But she had always been a very positive woman and had accepted the loss of one of her breasts extremely well. Furthermore, at sixty-four she liked the idea of her and Dad retiring and moving to Queensland, and it wasn't very long before someone bought her Mount Eliza fashion boutique. Then the house was put on the market and several people wanted to buy it so it sold almost immediately. Soon after, Mum and Dad decided to fly up and have a quick look for a house and Hayden and I were so excited.

I was still working at home with Suncoast Domestic Services when one morning, Michael called in on his way to work and said that he really needed a secretary. Unfortunately, he said that the owners of the shopping centre did not have anything in their budget to pay me but would let me run my own business from their office in return for me manning it full-time. There would also be some typing and other duties but not enough to interfere with the running of my business. I knew from experience that once I progressed into an office, the business would expand as it had in Melbourne and as I could not afford any rent, this would be a wonderful opportunity. After further discussion, Michael suggested that we have a trial period and as I had nothing to lose, I decided to give it a go.

All of a sudden it was Easter and I decided to test a theory I had about promoting Sugar Town. I asked Hayden to don an Easter Bunny suit and give out some small eggs supplied by the supermarket to children at the shopping centre. The tenants were thrilled as they had never had had any promotions before and were feeling the decline in customers since a new, more modern shopping centre, Ocean Breeze Plaza, had just opened two streets away.

I spoke to Michael about it and he said, 'If you could come up with something that would bring their old customers back and attract new ones, then maybe my friend Mr Abrahams could arrange some kind of payment for your trouble if it was a success.'

It was a slim chance but I was willing to try anything as my monthly allowance from Stan for Hayden had been temporarily stopped. He had recently had a stroke and as a result, could not work and unfortunately, he had to sell his portfolio of investment properties to prevent becoming bankrupt. He had lost nearly all of his money and was being cared for by one of his sisters as his mother had long passed away. His plan to make a fortune had been a waste of time and in a way, I felt very sorry for him.

One day, I dreamed up a promotion that would put Sugar Town back on track. As we had no stage, no centre court or anywhere at all to stage a live performance, I had to think of something feasible that we could do. I decided to make use of the antiquated design of the oblong car park, which was in the middle of all the shops. I figured that there must be some kind of aerial show that I could have above all the parked cars and verandas. I didn't have a clue what it would be until I saw a photo in a country newspaper of a man riding a motorbike over a high wire, with a pretty girl standing on his shoulders, at a local show. It looked very dangerous and I wondered if it was possible in our situation. After a myriad of phone calls, I managed to track him down. His name was Dare Devil Don, from the country, way out west, and he said that he would come and see me the following week. I told Michael of my idea and he was astonished and asked how I proposed to set up a high wire. I was prepared and replied that I had already got the green light from a company that had cranes for hire and they said all they would need was council approval and to speak to Dare Devil Don in person but they thought it would not be difficult.

After all the technical parts of the promotion had been worked out, I had the worst part ahead of me. I had to present the plan to the tenants, together with a budget. A meeting was duly convened by Michael and I explained that I was not charging them a cent for my services and I would be compering each performance on the roof of Chandlers, the electrical store. The tenants were all for it and did not mind chipping in with their fair share of the expenses.

But unfortunately, the next day Michael had bad news for me as he had to go Melbourne that week and would not be there to help me. I was going to be on my own but I didn't care.

I knew I could do it and I would succeed!

Soon, the week of my big promotion had arrived. I had notified all the TV stations and the press and I hoped and prayed that at least one would be interested in giving us the publicity that we needed. I had two shows daily for a week and after the first one, it was obvious that the crowds of people that attended were only interested in seeing Dare Devil Don and his lovely girlfriend, Ellie May, standing upright on his shoulders, fall off his bike. Little did they know that the wheels of the bike were hollow and narrow metal guards were secured around the cable and back onto the bike's wheels, so if the worst came to the worst, the bike would not fall down to the ground but just tip over and right itself. The riders each had safety harnesses also attached to the bike, so I wasn't at all worried. But from where the spectators stood, it appeared as if the bike and its occupants could come crashing down at any time. It did look hair-raising as the cable was situated above the shopping centre roof and Don was indeed the perfect daredevil. As a finale to the show, he did a loop the loop by himself and I increased the volume of the dramatic music that was booming all over the roofs of the shopping centre, and the crowds loved it.

Not one, but all the TV stations came to watch, and some had their helicopters hovering above taking footage of it. The press was marvellous also and I felt that all my hard work had been worth it, as the tenants were doing great business. I could not believe it when Friday afternoon arrived and it was the last show. The office phone rang and it was Mr Abrahams. He was very brief and said that he had seen coverage of my promotion on Melbourne television and wondered how many more shows I had left to do. I said that this was the last one, due to start in three minutes, and then he asked me to cancel it, if we, and the performers, did not have insurance. I nearly had a heart attack as I knew no one did. I immediately pretended that we had a bad line and hung up and took the phone off the hook.

I climbed out on the roof and compered the last show to a record crowd and extra traffic control police had to be put on point duty at the two exits and the surrounding streets.

Yippee! I had done it!

I went home thoroughly exhausted but on a high. I had done the impossible but my only worry was that the crowds would eventually taper off if I did not continue to promote Sugar Town. I felt a cold chill go up my spine when I thought of Mr Abraham's phone call.

Even though I had called him back after the show and told him of the safety precautions, he was not happy there had been no insurance and said that there was no excuse for this and would not have been tolerated if he had known prior to the event as it could have cost the shopping centre millions of dollars if an accident had occurred. I confessed that I had tried to get insurance for the promotion but not even Lloyds of London would touch it, so I had proceeded with my gut feeling but he didn't want to hear anymore and just hung up.

I realised then that I had cooked my own goose about earning any money from him, even though I had put his shopping centre on the map.

Still, I didn't care, as I had done my best and the tenants thought it was wonderful. I was happy with what I had done and knew that I had found my niche in the career world.

I wanted to work in shopping centre promotions and marketing, and one day, management.

It was so good to be home that evening but I was still caught up in all the day's hype and was looking forward to a quiet weekend when the phone rang. It was Stan and he sounded peculiar. He was now living by himself in a small unit and was trying to get back to normal after the stroke so that he could start contributing to Hayden's welfare again.

I thought that maybe he had had a set back with his health until he asked me if I was sitting down. He sounded very serious and so I sat down and then he said sadly, 'Lynne, I'm afraid there was an accident and Paul passed away this morning!'

I could not believe it and asked him how.

'When the staff was changing shifts and no one was looking, he absconded from his ward and ran out through the grounds and on to the Eastern Freeway and was run over twice. He was taken to St Vincent's Hospital but was dead on arrival.'

I burst into tears and started shaking. Hayden, of course, was worried and I had to break it to him as gently as I could. Thankfully, he took it well, as we all agreed it was the best thing for Paul as he was now at peace with God in heaven.

Next day, I bought a Melbourne paper with the death notice that Stan had written for us.

Paul Stanley [Result of accident]. The special son of Lynette and Stan, and Hayden's brother was cared for and protected since 1971 at the Kew Cottages, where he was treated with exceptional tenderness, warmth and love.
He was only a baby for sixteen years.
Thanks.

After reading it, I felt I had misjudged Stan and that he had really loved Paul in his own way but had not known how to cope with it.

I was already heartbroken, but these wonderful words of Stan's had just added fuel to the fire of my intense anguish and devastation.

Chapter 24

Flying High

Hayden and I flew down to Melbourne for Paul's funeral, which was held at the Holy Trinity Anglican Church, Kew and it was the saddest day of my life. I was a real mess. Stan came with his sister and her husband and of course, Sue was there and my church friends from Mount Eliza, Rev John with his wife Wendy, and all helped support Hayden and I. John officiated at the service and turned an extremely sad occasion into something beautiful and meaningful.

However, my heart broke when I saw the white coffin before the altar. It was a very private close family gathering and some of his devoted nurses from the Kew Cottages came. I was very touched by their attendance and I noticed that they were crying too. All I could do was to think of my endless love for my beloved Paul and to take comfort in that he was in God's care, free forever from the condition that had killed him and to know that from now on, he would always be safe.

After the funeral, Paul was laid to rest at the Templestowe Cemetery with a private service at his Graveside. It was a day I shall never forget.

The next day, Sue drove me back to Stan's unit to collect Hayden from his afternoon visit with his dad and I was utterly shocked at the condition of the inside of it. As Stan found it difficult to walk properly because of the stroke, housework obviously had been at the bottom of the list. When I had to go to the bathroom, I was greeted by mould growing everywhere and the toilet that had not been cleaned for weeks. It was quite obvious that Stan was not really ready to look after himself and had come home from his sister's place too early.

When we arrived back home in Queensland, Hayden immediately started missing his Dad terribly. It was probably a reaction exasperated by the loss of his brother whom of course, he had loved, and it worried me. I only had one son left and more than anything, I wanted him to be happy. I thought about it carefully for a few days. Stan needed looking after and we had the room, and even though we were divorced, I could not help feeling a moral obligation, both to Hayden and Stan. So after talking it over with Hayden, I decided to bite the bullet and invite Stan to come and stay with us indefinitely until he made a full recovery.

However, in the meantime, I had returned to work after my successful promotion. Suncoast Domestic Services had been neglected but I had to admit that my heart wasn't in it any more. My future, I believed, lay in promoting Sugar Town Shopping Centre and when I arrived at the office, I couldn't wait for Michael to say that surely I had been recognised for all my work. Unfortunately, it was not the case and I was so disappointed. I had put all that effort in promoting Sugar Town without getting a cent for it. I burst into tears and explained to Michael that I needed more money than I was making out of my agency now as Stan was coming to stay with us whilst he was recuperating, which could be a long time.

Michael was very sympathetic and said, 'I am so sorry, Lynne. Mr Abrahams said that as Sugar Town has no traders' association or promotions fund, there was no money available for you.'

I tried to put on a brave face and said, 'Oh well, at least I now know the reason why! But I am afraid that I will have to look elsewhere for a proper paying job, as I will soon have three mouths to feed, at my place.'

I easily found a job as a promotions manager for a new tourist attraction, Super Bee Honey Factory, as the manager had seen what I had done at Sugar Town and was impressed.

That afternoon, I went back to the office and packed up all my things as I had to start the next day. Michael was pleased that I had found a job so fast and I thanked him for the experience I had gained with him in his office. Then I made a snap decision to let him have Suncoast Domestic Services so that he could find someone else to man the office and help him as I had done as I didn't want to leave him in the lurch.

He was very grateful and so we had a big hug and said a sad goodbye.

As I walked out of Sugar Town, I could see that business was still brisk. The tenants were happy when they saw me and were still congratulating me on the promotion as I passed by. I was glad they didn't see the tears stinging in my eyes underneath my sunglasses as I smiled and waved to them for the last time.

The last fortnight had felt like the end of an era to me with darling Paul passing away, my working association with Michael ending and Stan arriving soon. My life had reached another turning point. Now more than ever, I was determined to succeed at Super Bee.

When Stan arrived, Hayden and I had our work cut out for us. I drove him to the beach early before I left for work each day as he attempted to walk on the sand, which I knew would be difficult for him, particularly in the soft sand. He started off poorly but after a few days, he improved dramatically. We also insisted that he squeeze an orange in his right hand as he watched television to improve his muscle co-ordination thus helping him to write again. After a while, he was doing really well and decided to do a correspondence course in real estate to give him the accreditation he needed to practice his real estate agent's licence in Queensland. We were so pleased to see him improving every day as he slowly regained his physical and mental confidence again.

One day, Mum rang full of excitement. At last, Mum and Dad had settled on a brand new house near Aimee and were moving in soon. They knew I was busy and she said not to worry about helping them as Aimee's husband, Clive, was retired and had offered to lend a hand. I was so thrilled for Mum as she had worked so hard all her life and never thought she would ever own a new home.

Over the past months, my job at Super Bee had been hard work but very rewarding and I loved it. I was hardly ever at home but it did not matter as Stan was always there after school for Hayden. I thought of numerous very successful promotions and they were all very well received and quite quickly, the visitor numbers increased due to my marketing strategies. Every week, I managed to have a photo and editorial published in the Sunshine Coast Daily newspaper until they started complaining that Super Bee was becoming overexposed. All of a sudden, I could see the writing on the wall. I had done a good job but had saturated the market. So I decided to move on before they moved me on.

My next job was as promotions manager of a radio station in Gympie. I had done the voiceovers for the advertisements that I had written for the tourist attraction and so I had got to know the manager at the studio when recording them. So when the position became vacant, he approached me and I was thrilled. A real bonus was the company supplying me with a Daihatsu four-wheel drive. I adored the job and spent the whole of the summer organising beach girl quests held on all the nearby beaches together with beach volleyball and the junior sand castle competitions for the children. Our sponsors provided us with wonderful prizes and I loved presenting them.

When summer ended, I had to conduct break dancing contests at tourist attractions, council parks and shopping centres.

Last on my list was the new Ocean Breeze Plaza close to Sugar Town and I went to the office to report to the centre manager, Mrs Angela Atkinson. She recognised me straight away and said, 'I've being trying to find you. I've never forgiven you for that aerial stunt you staged at Sugar Town. It made a real dent in our opening month's trading that week. Anyway, what are you doing working for a radio station, when you are really cut out for the shopping centre industry? I can see you managing your own centre one day. When can you start working for me?'

I was overwhelmed and managed to reply, saying, 'Oh, Mrs Atkinson, I would love to start as soon as possible. I will give the station a week's notice immediately. Thank you so much.'

I was elated as now at long last, I would be doing exactly what I really wanted to do.

When I got home, Stan had some good news also. Having recently completed the Queensland accreditation for his real estate qualifications, he had managed to sell his full real estate agent's licence to a company in Maroochydore. Part of the deal was that the company had to employ him for twelve months. I was so pleased for him as that was just the start that Stan needed to get back on his feet. Now that his health was back to normal, I realised that he would be moving out soon, which for me, would be something to look forward to in more ways than one.

Every time I had been going out with a new male friend, it had been embarrassing for all parties when I had been picked up at home and had to introduce my escort to my ex-husband, who just happened to live there with me. Sometimes it had been hard to convince my suitors that I had a teenage son and that there were three bedrooms in the unit, all of which were occupied by one person only.

I was in my element at Ocean Breeze. Angela Atkinson was a hard taskmaster, but she trained me well and sent me to some BOMA (Building Owners and Managers Association) shopping centre management courses. I had a natural talent of a huge imagination for fresh new ideas but of course, I needed professional training in all facets of this industry. I was so fortunate to have Angela as my mentor as well, which gave me an excellent grounding for my next twenty years that I was to spend working in shopping centres. It was lucky that I was experienced with using a microphone and loved compering live shows and fashion parades. I really enjoyed my work and was popular with the tenants.

I had gone over to Sugar Town several times to tell Michael of my new job but his office had always been shut. Strangely, the girl he had found to take over from me was not there either and so I asked the tenants in the delicatessen what was going on. They said that Sugar Town had recently been sold and the new owners already had a full-time centre manager so Michael had been let go. He had decided to buy a Beachfront Resort somewhere on the Capricorn Coast but had to move there as soon as possible.

I was very surprised and really hoped that he would like it.

Suddenly, I felt all alone, as now I would have to give up the gourmet circle and so decided to advertise in the personal column of the Brisbane Courier Mail for an _unattached_ gentleman companion.

To my surprise, I received thirty-five answers. My post office box was stuffed with letters every day for a week and a half and I was amazed. I had great fun sifting through them and met a few that lived close by but unfortunately, none were suitable or lived too far away, making it geographically impossible for me to consider them. However, there was still one letter left that I had liked the sound of, and had answered, but I had not heard a word from him for six weeks and so had almost given up hope. Then one day, totally unexpected, he phoned me at work and I had to think very hard when Barbara, our receptionist, said there was a George Carter on the line. We had a short conversation and he said that if I liked, he would pick me up next Monday on my day off and take me to lunch. I was surprised and impressed as he sounded like a very polite gentleman and so I agreed. The girls in the office had pricked up their ears and were intrigued that a new man was about to come into my life but not half as much as I was.

Monday arrived and at the appointed time, a Blue Rolls Royce appeared out the front of my unit. George had driven up from the Gold Coast where he lived and came to the front door with a bunch of flowers. I was thrilled and liked him immediately. As we got going, I felt like a queen as George had opened the car door for me and then helped fasten my seat belt. I felt really special as we drove through Coolum and the Rolls floated along like a dream. We had about three-quarters of an hour to get to know one another before we arrived in the Hinterland at Montville. He stopped at a beautiful old stone restaurant where the gourmet club had been to once but that had been at night. The owner remembered me and winked as she showed us to our table.

It was a perfect lunch but surprisingly, we were the only ones there. As we left, I commented on the fact that it was a shame for the owner that no one else had patronised her restaurant but George just laughed and said, 'I didn't want anyone else here! I wanted to get to know you without any distractions, so I booked the whole place just for us.'

I was overwhelmed and quite flattered.

The time had flown and suddenly we were back at my front door. George then asked me if I would like to go to Fraser Island for lunch at Orchid Beach next week. I was puzzled as it would take almost a day to drive up there along the beaches in a four-wheel drive. I thought that as he was coming from the Gold Coast, it would be impossible. Again he laughed and said, 'No worries,

Lynne. It won't take us long to fly up from Maroochydore to the resort. I've got a twin-engine Bravo Blue Comanche aeroplane that will get us there in no time. What do you think?'

I nodded yes enthusiastically and he gave me a shy little kiss, with closed lips, and drove away.

It always showed when I had a good man in my life and so my work at Ocean Breeze exceeded all expectations. This, unfortunately for me, made my boss Angela become jealous of my abilities and results. The tenants were making it clear that they would rather deal with me than her and things were becoming awkward. I was a bit worried as my contract had been for a year and was nearly up. I needed permanent work, of course, so I decided to keep my eyes open.

We had monthly meetings with other shopping centre managers and marketing managers on the Coast and were due for one the following week, so I took the opportunity to cautiously put out a feeler or two, which in the end paid off.

Meanwhile, I couldn't wait for my next date with George as that was sure to take my mind off any negative thoughts at work. I was so keen that on the day, I got to the airport earlier than I needed to. It was interesting going to where all the light private aircrafts landed and were housed. Some of the planes, like a four-seater single-engine Cessna, looked not much bigger than a car with wings. I was very glad that we were not going in something like that. All at once, I saw George waving and standing near quite a large, very smart-looking blue plane with curtains to match. It was indeed a twin-engine plane and really looked like a *Blue Bird of Happiness*, ready for us to fly up into the perfect cloudless sky and I was rapt.

George helped me inside sitting next to him and away we went. I was so enamoured with his expertise although he kept saying that flying was easy. After we had cleared the airport and were out to sea, he asked me if I would like to have a flying lesson. Inside, I was petrified but not wanting to seem like a scaredy cat, I said yes. It really wasn't that hard at all and in fact, I actually got a kick out of it. George explained that the hardest part of flying a plane was taking off and landing. When I had had enough and we were getting close to our destination, he took over the controls and I noted George's skilful landing on the tiny airstrip, and experienced a growing feeling of admiration for him. The restaurant was at the resort on the north-eastern side of the island and right on the beach. We had a delightful lunch sitting on the veranda outside with a gorgeous sea view.

I was allowed alcohol as I was not the pilot but George had to abstain. He didn't mind as he was used to it but he did not stop me from having the best champagne so I made the most of it.

Flying back to Maroochydore seemed so easy and George put the plane on autopilot. Then he asked me if I had ever joined the Mile High Club. I had never heard of it and asked George to tell me about it.

'Lynne, you are such a sweet girl. Fancy not hearing about the Mile High Club! It means having sex in the air. Would you like to try it?'

I was amazed and eagerly replied, 'As you virtually have me as a prisoner here, I might as well lie back and think of England, so they say, and enjoy it.' And we both smiled as he down bent to kiss me. Secretly, I was looking forward to it. The two glasses of champagne I had at lunch were making me feel sexy anyway and before I knew it, I had one of the most powerful orgasms I had ever had in my life.

I felt lighter than air. It was incredible!

Chapter 25

New Beginnings

Back at work, I had given Angela a month's notice as I would not be seeking to renew my contract with Ocean Breeze. I could tell that, in a way, she was pleased that I was going but also concerned that I was going to Seaside Central, a large established centre, which was on the perimeter of Ocean Breeze's customer catchment area. Although I had made a name for myself at Ocean Breeze, I was determined to do even better at Seaside Central and I think she sensed I could be a real threat.

Mum and Dad had settled in very well living in Peregian Beach and it had helped having Aimee and Clive as close neighbours. My parents were so happy and like a young couple again, starting out on a new adventure. It didn't take them long to create a beautiful garden and to join the local lawn bowling club. Their lives had really changed for the better, except that I knew they missed Sue and the girls. However, as school holidays were around the corner, they knew that they would be coming up and staying with them.

Our first family Sunday roast dinner with Hayden and me at Mum and Dad's new house was delightful. Dad had had a swimming pool built for Mum as she was feeling the heat and we all took advantage of it. Mum enjoyed cooking a feast in her new kitchen and said that moving to Queensland was the best thing they had ever done.

A few weeks later, we were at the Maroochydore Airport waiting for the small Qantas Link connecting plane from Brisbane with its precious passengers on board to land. We were all so excited to see Sue, Bridie and Myffy, descend down the steps and quickly walk over the tarmac. It was so good to see them again. I had missed them all so much but of course that was the penalty for living interstate.

I was still with Ocean Breeze and had recently traded in the Volvo for a new little yellow Suzuki Sierra, a four-wheel drive vehicle. I had taken it on the beach a few times so I knew the ropes for when I took Sue and the girls for a picnic. It was a perfect day and the first thing we had to do was make sure that we had a full tank of petrol as we were going to drive up the beach along the sand to Double Island Point. There was great excitement as we waited for our turn to board the barge and cross the beautiful Noosa River. Sue remarked how clear and blue the water was, compared with the Yarra River in Melbourne. The girls were intrigued with my bull bar and fishing rods in their holders on the front of the vehicle and I told them that I was going to teach them how to catch a fish.

The track from the other side of the river was rough but we bumped along merrily and soon made it to the first cutting and on to the sand dunes. I hopped out and changed the wheels into the freewheeling mode and put the car gear into four-wheel drive. Then I told everyone to hang on as we sailed over the soft dunes and made it on to the hard sand near the ocean, which was a big relief. The little Suzuki rode smoother on this sand than it did on bitumen and we were soon in another world. The sun was shining on the surf as we sailed by and after about ten minutes, we stopped and had a cool drink. There were not many people around as it was a Monday, which was my day off, but it was the school holidays. It was so unspoilt and pristine. Sue loved it and began to relax as she had been working very hard this term being a Year 12 English teacher.

We passed by the Teewah Beach fishing village, where there were a few secluded holiday shacks in the dunes but there was no electricity or water connected there. It was very remote. We stopped at everything of interest including the Coloured Sands, which were layers of different coloured sand in the cliffs bordering the National Park.

Then I told them to keep their eyes peeled straight ahead for a ship in the sand. They thought I was joking until they saw the remains of *The Cherry Venture*, a ship that had been blown off course and beached there several years before. We all got out and went exploring. Even though it was rusted, there were still spots of paint remaining and it was quite safe to climb on. My camera was busy taking shots when Yummy, the local ice cream vendor, came along beside us in his dune buggy, which was of course named *Yummy's Ice Cold Refreshments*. He knew me from fishing on my days off and I introduced him to everyone. Ice cream never tasted so good as it did out in the middle of nowhere on a superb beach.

In another ten minutes, we had reached our destination and saw the Double Island Point Light House and I found the perfect spot to park the vehicle under some shady trees, a stone's throw away from the water. We had a swim and then had lunch. It was fantastic and Sue had been so intrigued to hear about my latest friend George. Then we went fishing and I made sure that with my help, everyone caught a fish in one of the low-tide pools.

Suddenly, Myffy alerted us to a beautiful dog walking along the shore and I told her and Bridie not to go near it as it was a dingo and although it looked tame, it was really a wild animal. As I loved dogs, I said that I would leave the scraps from our cold chicken for him on the beach when we left but of course, now it is illegal to feed them.

The whole day had been one that we would never forget.

We were all so happy, and I realised just how much I loved my sister and her darling girls and I hoped that they would be back in the Christmas holidays.

Stan had just moved out. He was doing well at his job and had bought a second-hand car and put a small deposit on a unit in Mooloolaba whilst I had been busy at work winding up all my last promotions before I started my new job.

The centre manager of Seaside Central was a real tyrant. Derrick Warner was a perfectionist and very moody. The girls in the office were terrified of him and were quick to warn me. Fortunately, I got on well with him and he soon suggested that I attend Shopping Centre Marketing No.1, which was a course held once a year at the University of Administration in Sydney. It was extremely expensive but thankfully, the Kern Corporation, the company that owned the centre, paid for me. It was a very arduous week but I managed to come home triumphantly with my hard-earned qualifications. I had met a lot of interesting people who were in the shopping centre industry and I now felt part of it as many of my colleagues were working in Queensland centres and we had become friends.

My social life had been on hold for a while but luckily, I had been so intent on doing my best at Seaside Central. George had temporarily faded out of the picture as being an importer of top-named sporting goods, including tennis rackets, clothing, caps and shoes, he seemed to be always busy overseas. However, my holidays were looming up and we had made arrangements to go sailing on his yacht in the Whitsundays for a week and I was looking forward to it.

Meanwhile, one day I was delivering memos to the tenants and was chatting with Helen from the photoshop when she told me about her wonderful doctor, Dr Applegate, who had found a cure for her sick daughter when others had failed. I normally did not have much time to spare listening to their stories but I always made a point of asking every tenant how they were. Just as I was leaving, however, my curiosity got the better of me and I asked her the Christian name of her doctor.

When she said it was Stewart, I nearly died!

I asked her if he had lived here long and she said that it had only been a year or so and that he had come from Tasmania. I could not believe it. Then I said to her casually that I thought I knew him from when I lived in Victoria and she said that she would ask him if he remembered me.

For the rest of the day, my mind went into overdrive. I wondered why on Earth I was so concerned about it and then Derrick reprimanded me for not hurrying with my latest report.

A week passed by and Helen came rushing up to me as I entered her shop. She said that Dr Applegate did remember me and would probably see me on Saturday morning as he was planning to come to the centre's motor show display that I was running. I thanked her and tried hard to conceal my feelings of excitement and anticipation.

Saturday morning came and I made sure that I was wearing my most flattering outfit. I had washed and carefully styled my long blond hair and had even sprayed myself with Stewart's favourite perfume. I wondered if he was happy with his life and how his second marriage with Grace had worked out. I was amazed that I still had feelings for him after all these years.

Unfortunately, all my hopes of seeing him again were dashed when he didn't show up.

I had almost worn out a pair of stiletto-heeled shoes that morning, walking from one end of the centre to the other looking for him.

When it was closing time at the end of the day, I knew that he wasn't coming and I went home feeling let down and quite upset.

Next time I saw Helen, I told her that Stewart had not come on the Saturday morning and she seemed quite strange and agitated. I actually got the feeling that she didn't want to talk about it. She said that she was sure he must have had a very good reason but somehow, it didn't ring true. Then I wondered what she had told him. Maybe at the last minute she had said that I didn't want to see him. I didn't know what to make of it and probably never would.

It was so frustrating. It was almost as if she had a bit of crush on him herself as I knew he was so charismatic.

I felt like making an appointment to see him at his surgery but then I realised that that would be ridiculous and maybe I should just let sleeping dogs lie.

Meanwhile, I had better things to think of. My holiday with George started off with a return ticket to Hamilton Island waiting for me at Brisbane Airport. Mum and Dad were minding Hayden and so I decided to forget about everything and just have a good time. I wasn't disappointed as George's stylish motor cruiser was the smartest boat in the marina. The interior was all teak and it had every luxury, including marble bathrooms. I loved it, even before we set sail. I learnt a lot from George, who very generously let me take the wheel for short periods every day until I had my confidence. He reminded me a bit of the film star Brian Brown in many ways. Apart from his looks, he was a true-blue Aussie, who would give you the shirt off his back if you needed it.

In other words, his money was not the real reason I liked him.

I thought it was fantastic to be able to anchor wherever we chose and then go ashore in the dinghy and have a picnic on a deserted beach. We had television but only watched the news and the weather report each evening as we mainly sat on the upper deck and had a peaceful dinner with fine wine under the stars.

We seemed to be getting closer and I wondered where it was all going to lead. I had a funny feeling that it was not going to be permanent and so on our last night, I asked George if he was married. He said that he had been waiting for me to ask him and that he was married, and had been for thirty-five years but his wife had not been interested in sex since the onset of menopause. Then he said it was the first time he had ever strayed and that he was a Catholic. It sounded like a broken record to me but I did believe him. After all, it wasn't his fault that I had not asked him earlier in our friendship. I still cared for him though and at this stage, I didn't want anything to spoil what was left of our holiday, so I suggested that we go to bed early and make the most of our last night.

The holiday had done me good physically and I came back to work with renewed vigour before the busy Christmas period. But mentally, of course, I was still upset after finding out that George was married. I had no choice but to end our relationship, much to his dismay. I felt really disappointed as yet another prospective husband had turned out to be unavailable. So I decided to throw myself into my work and try to forget all about men for a while.

The previous Christmas, I had arranged for Santa's arrival at Seaside Central in a silver sleigh on wheels pulled along by a team of beautiful white Samoyed dogs. It was a great hit and our centre got all the publicity as the Santa at Ocean Breeze decided not to have an official welcome. So this year, I had to think of something really different as I knew Angela, who had been so furious with me last year, would be determined to top any promotion I presented. Derrick was impressed with my format for this year and gave me the green light.

I was so resolute that I put forward Santa's traditional arrival date by a week and flooded the media with advance notice of my promotion.

The magical day came and Santa arrived by camel, paraded from the highway along the car park driveway, up to the front entrance where hundreds of people were waiting. Then he was helped down by the camel's keeper who led the animal away to a waiting truck.

Meanwhile, Santa was made a pillion passenger aboard a brand-new Harley Davison. Enthralled, wide-eyed children could not believe it all when the motorbike engine revved up as Santa was driven away inside the centre to his special chair on the stage and all the parents and kids followed madly.

We got a front-page photo in the press and it was featured on all the local news TV services.

Ocean Breeze had their Santa arrival a week later and it was regarded as old news and not rated a mention. Ours had been a huge success and Derrick was thrilled. As a reward, he enrolled me in another university course for early next year, but this time it was for shopping centre management. He had also given me the title of assistant centre manager and I was very flattered, as I could see that I was progressing up the corporate ladder from marketing to management.

However, I was getting very tired of Derrick taking all the credit for my ideas.

After the course the following year, my work became more intense as I was being groomed by the company to be a centre manager in one of their other centres. I was fortunate that they had faith in my ability but I really did not want to move away from the Sunshine Coast.

So, one day, I applied for a job at a new exciting shopping centre to be called Bayside Mall. It was very upmarket and I loved the sound of it. In the industry, it was known as a resort leisure centre as opposed to a regional shopping centre with supermarkets and discount department stores.

I got the job and the owner wanted a grand opening, which was right up my alley.

At last, I was going to be a shopping centre manager!

Derrick was not amused. He would have to think up his own promotions now.

However, he felt he had to have an early farewell party for me and all the tenants wanted to wish me well but Helen from the photoshop looked especially worried and started sprouting tears, so I asked her what was wrong, thinking of her sick daughter. Then she told me that she felt bad as she had never told me the real reason why Dr Applegate had not come to see me at the motor show. On that particular morning, his wife Grace had died after collapsing on their kitchen floor with an aneurism.

When Helen had found out, she was too upset to talk about it to me. However, that was three months ago and as I was leaving, she felt it her duty to tell me about it now. I was so shocked. Then I asked how Stewart was taking it and she said he was broken-hearted and that the next day he was leaving Australia to go back home to England for good.

I couldn't believe it!

It was like I had been playing some kind of never ending see-saw game over the years, and I had finally just been struck out for the last time. The first time had been with Zelda, the second time with Grace, and now the third time with England! I decided then and there that I had had enough of it and would put it to rest forever before it destroyed me once more. It was now going to be ancient history and I breathed a sigh of relief.

Chapter 26

Unexpected Surprises

All of a sudden Hayden made a mammoth decision to live with Stan and take on a carpet cleaning business that his father had financed for him. I had my work cut out planning a sensational opening for the new Bayside Mall, and so this lessened the loneliness I felt after he left home.

The opening was a huge undertaking but I succeeded in staging the most impressive opening of commercial premises that the Coast had ever seen. It was held at night and the centre was all lit up and looked magical. I interviewed visiting famous TV stars on stage and had a string quartet and red roses with perfume samples attached to the stems for all the ladies. Also, I compered a fashion parade held on the indoor/outdoor curved staircase steps, surrounded in a background of coloured fog from a smoke machine, spotlights on the models and modern music. I ended it with the new advertising jingle for the centre that I had made into a recording for advertising.

My boss was the landlord and generously had provided hot nibbles and free drinks for a crowd of over two hundred invited guests. We had opened with a bang and it was the talk of the town for ages. I was thrilled and survived on nervous energy and needed a short break.

So it was good timing when Sue and the girls were up again and they all stayed with me. Sue and I enjoyed our happy hours every night and she was very intrigued to hear all about the final ending of George and also the Stewart Applegate saga.

On day two, we decided to go up the beach and try out my new larger, second-hand four-wheel drive vehicle which was a red Holden Drover.

As we were getting ready to go and Sue was changing into her bathers, I noticed quite a pronounced lump on one of her breasts. She didn't seem to be worried about it and said that as it didn't hurt, she had ignored it and in any case, it had been there for a long time. However, I was not convinced that it should be ignored and made her promise to have it checked when she got back home. The discovery of the lump had put a dampener on the day for me as I thought of Mum's mastectomy but as Sue and the girls were having such a lovely time, I temporarily put it out of my mind. My sister was having a ball, catching small whiting and the girls were thrilled at how many pippy shell fish they were finding for bait in the sand at the water's edge.

The day finished with Hayden joining us at Mum and Dad's for a family roast. The girls loved Hayden and he adored them. As we sat down to eat, Myf, as she now liked to call herself, and Hayden started clowning around and Dad lost his temper. He blamed Hayden for teasing Myf and suddenly grabbed him by the arm and thumped him. Hayden could have fought back and easily won but he just calmly said that he would never speak to his grandfather ever again, and left the room. The evening had ended abruptly and upset everyone. Just when I thought Dad had mellowed, he had reverted back to his old ways. Sue and I looked at each other and remembered the episode with the pillow and poor little Paul.

Next day, our visitors flew home and I relayed my fears to Mum about Sue's lump. We both prayed for good news. But it wasn't.

She had to have her right breast taken off immediately and chemotherapy had been ordered to follow. I was devastated! How dare this happen to my beautiful little sister!

In a few months after all the treatment was over, Sue and the girls came up again for another holiday. Due to her treatment, Sue's gorgeous blonde hair had fallen out and was being replaced by a mousy regrowth. Her face was also puffed up as a side effect from medication and my heart went out to her and the girls and Dick. Nevertheless, I decided to treat her normally as I had always done and that night, a few gin and tonics were definitely in order.

No doctor had any idea of a prognosis and as Mum had gone on for years after her mastectomy, it was not brought up. The main thing was that she was alive and as well as could be expected so we planned yet another picnic up the beach.

It was a very hot day and Sue seemed to feel the heat more than ever before. She had always had very fair skin and been careful not to expose herself to the sun for long periods but this time she seemed to burn very easily, just sitting near the car window for twenty minutes. I did not go far along the beach as I was a bit nervous that she may get tired but we had a lovely time just the same. Unfortunately, Sue got sunburnt even though she had been very careful and sat in the shade all the time. I felt responsible as that night was most uncomfortable for her, even with all our tried-and-true home sunburn remedies.

After a day or so, she was back to normal, thank goodness, but from then on we took no chances with her in the sun. Before dinner, we continued to have our gin and tonics each evening but Sue did not speak of the future, or even what she had gone through with the operation and the treatment. As she did not broach the subject, I took the hint and did not mention anything about it either. The last thing I wanted to do was upset her. I thought that it must be very difficult trying to deal with something unknown and I supposed that only time would tell what would happen. I had the utmost admiration for my little sister and prayed that she would come through this horrible experience. When it was time for them to go back to Melbourne, Mum, Dad, Hayden and I were at the airport to say goodbye and just managed to keep the tears back until they were aboard the plane. We felt so helpless and it was at times like these that we wished we did not live so far away from them.

Back at work, one afternoon when I was out doing the banking for Bayside Mall, I bumped into Allison, the secretary from Pacific Palms Shopping Centre. It was a picturesque open-air centre with a real tropical feel. Of course, it had palm trees everywhere and colourful bougainvillea in the gardens around the verandas and fishponds. Apart from being a regional centre, it was almost a tourist attraction in itself. I knew Allison, or Ally, as she was known, through the combined shopping centre monthly meetings we attended. She was very excited and said that her boss had decided to leave and maybe I would like to put in for the position. I was so pleased that she told me as I had always wanted to manage Pacific Palms, so I decided to apply immediately.

Imagine my surprise and delight when after a gruelling interview in Brisbane from the chauvinistic managing agents, I got the job.

My first day at Pacific Palms went extremely well, as Ally and I got on like a house on fire. I had never had my own secretary before and Ally soon learnt how to make my coffee just right. She was a beautiful-looking girl, with a lovely, kind nature to go with it. Originally from a big country town way out west where she had worked at a TAB, she was a wiz at figures, which was my weakness and so she was a huge help to me. I had reached the top of the ladder of my ambition and I wanted my career to peak at Pacific Palms, but I realised that because I was a woman in a male-dominated profession, I had to prove myself yet again.

The first thing I did was to introduce myself to the tenants, then the cleaner, gardener and all the tradespeople that serviced the centre.

I spent the whole of the week asking questions of what in their opinion needed doing to improve and maintain the upkeep of the buildings and the property. I got to know the plumbing, air conditioning and electrical contractors first, and then looked at the annual budget, which was due to be compiled for the coming financial year. Apart from all of this, accounts had to be approved for payment by me and sent down to the managing agents to be paid. The Traders Association, which was responsible for the payment of promotions, I discovered, was on the verge of being sued for outstanding advertising debts. I had my hands full but what a challenge! I loved it.

The Traders Association Committee Members were horrified when I held a meeting and told them of my discovery regarding their promotions fund. The problem had arisen as the sales representative from the Coast newspaper had approached each tenant and talked some of them into buying a full page of advertising space, and then getting another space the same size free, which of course would be subsidised by our Traders Association by fifty per cent and the paper the other fifty per cent. In other words, it was an open-ended offer but some tenants, who didn't advertise at all were helping to pay for tenants who did and as a result, the Traders Association's money had soon run out and then the paper and other companies had now threatened legal action for unpaid bills.

At a meeting of the Traders Association Committee, I said that I would have a creditors' meeting and sort out the problems but it would mean that only promotions that did not cost the centre any money would occur until we became solvent again.

As I had had experience working on a shoestring, I knew that we could do it and I put forward a promotional calendar for the next few months and they were impressed.

After the next meeting, most of the sceptical male members suddenly became good friends and from then on, my work at Pacific Palms became easier as they got to know me and despite being a female, I earned their respect.

Ally said that the owner of the centre, Mr Barclay, had a house in Sydney but because of business commitments, he was based in Hong Kong for most of the time. So it came as a complete surprise when the managing agents of the centre in Brisbane faxed us to let us know that Mr Barclay was making a special trip soon to meet me, his new centre manager. I had a terrible feeling that he could be a male chauvinist and I was in for a bad time but Ally told me that he was a very nice gentleman and not to worry. He usually flew down from Hong Kong a few times of the year to inspect his Australian properties. However, I couldn't help feeling nervous.

The night before he arrived, I couldn't sleep but Ally was right. When Mr Barclay did arrive, he knocked on the office sliding glass door. I nearly had heart failure. He was so polite and waited for Ally to open the door and let him in, even though he owned the place.

Oh my goodness! He was the man of my dreams. Suddenly, I was in love, at first sight!

He came inside the office and greeted Ally and then she formally introduced me to him. He was impeccably dressed and spoke like English royalty. When he shook my hand, he smiled at me and the corners of his blue eyes turned upwards. He was a lovely man. I felt an instant exchange of chemistry between us and I wondered if it was all in my imagination but I didn't think so. It was quite unexpected and something that I had been totally unprepared for.

The day was exhausting as Mr Barclay did his best to test my ability to manage to his centre. Luckily I had all the answers for him and ended up taking him on a tour of inspection, pointing out various problems that needed attention. Finally, I took him out up on to the roof to inspect the air conditioning unit and showed him the housing that should be painted to prevent the motors from rusting in the salt air. He seemed to be impressed with my sound knowledge of the centre in such a short time and then asked to see how the annual budget preparation was coming along. To my surprise, he sat down with me in my office at the boardroom table where I was working and helped me with it.

We got along so well and when it was time to go home, he said, 'I hope you don't mind me calling you Lynne?'

I smiled and said, 'It's much better than Lynette.'

Then he said, 'Would you like to come out and have a drink with me at my hotel on your way home? You can call me Rob, if you like.'

Wow! I couldn't believe my ears but even though I would have loved to accept his offer, I decided to refuse. After all, he was my boss and maybe he was testing my business ethics. He seemed disappointed and asked me to reconsider. Again, I declined and so regretfully, he gave up.

The next day I was at the office early but it wasn't long before Rob arrived, ready to start work again with me. He was amazed when I told him about the Traders Association being in so much debt. Then he congratulated me on the way I had handled things. We continued working hard all morning and Ally kept making coffee for us and then brought in sandwiches for us all at lunchtime.

It had been another full day but I was thriving on it. I had the best teacher I could possibly wish for. He was a very intelligent man and I learnt so many things from him. Then all at once, it was the end of the day and Rob said, 'Lynne, I was sorry that you didn't come last night for that drink with me as I had to go back to the hotel on my own. I would very much like it if you would consider dining with me tonight. I could pick you up at seven.'

I couldn't resist any longer and so I decided to go for it.

We had a wonderful night. Strangely, it seemed as if we had known each other forever.

I couldn't believe it. It seemed so right for me.

We were both in high spirits and when Rob politely kissed me goodnight on my hand, I could tell that both of us found it hard just to leave it at that.

The next day was Rob's last day. He had an appointment with the bank manager early in the morning so I took the chance to tell Ally what was going on. She reminded me a bit of Sue, who was always interested in my romances. Of course, it was no surprise to her as she could tell that I had liked Rob from the beginning but she had no idea that he had invited me out and that the feeling could be mutual between us. She hesitated and then spoke to me like a concerned sister. She started cautiously saying that she thought he might be too old for me. I replied by saying I knew he was sixty and as I was forty-seven, there was only a thirteen-year difference between us. I could tell that she was disappointed that I was still keen and so she gently dropped the bombshell that he was married. I was shocked and said that I would sort it all out before it got serious. Secretly though, I knew that it was serious already and I didn't want it to end, and I wondered what on Earth was I going to do.

That night, I decided to invite Rob for dinner at my place as it was his birthday. He was most surprised that I did not want to go out to an expensive restaurant, which is what he had suggested. I ran through my specialties that I knew men liked and he requested lamb's fry and bacon with mashed potatoes and green peas. The day at the office flew by as he was only there for half of it and he gave me an early mark to go home and prepare the meal.

He arrived on the dot of seven and we had drinks out on the deck with my romantic Brazilian cassette music softly playing 'The Girl from Ipanema' in the background. It was an evening to remember and after some wine, he suddenly volunteered the information I had dreaded hearing.

The story was that he was not happy at home and had not been happy for a long time. Years ago, his family and his wife's family, who were friends, decided to match-make and arrange the marriage. The only thing stopping him from a divorce now that the children had grown up was his conscience, but up until now, he had not found the right woman. We danced very closely in between courses. He loved the food and the company and of course, one thing led to another.

It seemed a natural progression and it was a perfect union. I had never had anything like it. We were momentarily fused together by an inexplicable electrical force and then near the end, it was if we were no longer encased in our bodies as it was our souls that had melded together somewhere in paradise. It was almost like an out-of-this-world experience of euphoria and one filled with deep reverence. It was so beautiful and as we were coming back down to Earth, I knew that it would be unforgettable.

Rob left at five in the morning and went straight to the airport. I was half asleep when he went and it was only much later when I got up that I noticed that he had left his birthday card behind on the kitchen bench. I had wished him a happy birthday and taken a risk and expressed my love in the card, and so I thought that under the circumstances, he would not want it to get into the wrong hands. I read it again and saw that underneath my writing, he had written that he was in love with me too. My heart was thumping.

I had found my soul mate! But I wondered, at what price?

When I arrived at the office, I asked Ally to make us a cup of coffee. We sat down for our usual morning briefing, which of course was a mixture of business and gossip. When she had finished telling me her news, I made her swear to secrecy and then confessed as to what had transpired the night before. Ally couldn't believe it and as I was still in a delirious daze, it seemed unreal to me also. She was amazed when I told her what Rob had written on the birthday card but then she quickly added that she hoped I was not going to get hurt. However, as I was the eternal optimist, I said that it was all in God's hands and that one day, Rob could be mine. She smiled sweetly and then gave me a sisterly hug. I was so lucky to have her as above all, I knew that I could trust her and tell her anything without the whole world knowing.

It was hard to switch off what had happened in the last few days but I now had even more of a desire to make Pacific Palms the best shopping centre on the Sunshine Coast. Top of my list was Santa's arrival for Christmas. The media was expecting great things from me and I was determined not to let them down. Even though it was only September, I had to start planning every detail.

I was so pleased that Ally was a wonderful gardener. I appreciated other people's gardens but I hardly knew the difference between weeds and plants. However, I knew about maintenance as being a single parent for a number of years, I had to learn to become a Jill of All Trades. So Ally and I had a meeting with the cleaner, Fred, and the gardener, Joe, and between the four of us had the centre looking beautiful and clean in no time. I must confess that I did not envy Fred and Joe's weekend task that I had set them of emptying the water in the fishponds and cleaning them out. They were experts at it and I am pleased to say managed to save all the goldfish. After they had finished, the accolades from the public made it clear that we were on the right track.

After that success, there was no stopping me in making improvements and the next was the car park and its traffic flow. I worked nonstop on every facet over and above my job specification, and completed a SWOT exercise. This was, of course, a report on the centre's strengths, weaknesses, opportunities and threats, which I planned to hand to Rob personally on his next visit.

I used to come home every night worn out but fulfilled. I was happy until one night I had a phone call from Sue. I was immediately concerned as she didn't sound like her usual herself. I had been worried ever since her mastectomy and was hoping that she had seen the end of it all.

Unfortunately, it was not the case. It was now apparent that the surgeon had not been able to contain the cancer and it had spread to her bones.

We both knew what this meant. It was a death sentence.

She was only forty-two!

He had to be wrong! It had to be a mistake! But she assured me it wasn't!

She only had months left to live!

Chapter 27

Things Happen In Threes

At work, we got a memo faxed from the managing agents telling us that Mr Barclay would be visiting the centre again and to make sure that everything was shipshape. I was so excited that he was coming but Ally warned me not to be disappointed if he had had a change of heart during his absence. I said that in my case, absence had made my heart grow fonder! She smiled and said that she hoped everything would turn out alright.

Then suddenly there was a knock on the door, and there he was! Ally and I got such a surprise that he had arrived already and I couldn't wait until the day ended so that I could talk about things, other than work. Rob was very complimentary about all the changes I had made to the centre but I made sure that Ally got the credit for her help and support and especially her gardening input. It was a very difficult day in one way, as Rob and I had to be business-like and in fact, I hoped that he had not had second thoughts, as he seemed to be quite remote. But of course, Rob had no idea that Ally had the slightest suspicion of our feelings and I supposed that he was just being careful. I spent the afternoon presenting my SWOT exercise and Rob decided to adopt all of my recommendations. It was very exciting as he enlarged on some of my original ideas and we drew up a rough capital expenditure budget.

At long last, it was time to go home and we said goodbye to Ally. Next moment, Rob locked the outer door and we went into my office and shut the door. As our lips met, we both experienced a sharp spark of electricity and instantly pulled back. Nothing like that had ever happened to either of us before. We knew that we were both charged up and had been waiting for a moment to be alone together all day but this was unbelievable. It was a shock to us, in more ways than one. However, the second kiss proceeded normally and was the one that I had remembered and had been longing for in my heart. I was back in outer space!

Before he left for Hong Kong, Rob expressed a desire to meet my parents. I was taken aback as none of my previous male friends had ever mentioned them, let alone wanted to meet them. However, I thought it was very honourable of him and it demonstrated to me that he was serious about our relationship. I felt a bit nervous bringing him home but I need not have worried. Mum had gone to a lot of trouble making her famous date scones and a cream sponge, both of which Rob enjoyed and he gave Mum glowing compliments. They were Dad's favourites also and I was so relieved that he and Rob seemed to be getting on so well. Then Rob asked about all the family photos around the room. When he came to Sue's photo, Dad broke the news that her condition had worsened and that she was no longer allowed to even lift a litre carton of milk as it would break a bone. Dad was heartbroken and Rob was immediately sympathetic. As we were leaving and walking down the drive, Rob went back and spoke to Mum privately for a minute. It wasn't until the next time I saw Mum that I found out what he had said to her. Apparently Rob had promised her, that he would always look after me.

Oh! My goodness!

My Christmas promotion at the centre was very successful. I had always liked aerial spectaculars and luckily I found Leo, a man complete with a Santa suit who was prepared to arrive by helicopter at a reasonable rate.

Leo made a grand entrance and the chopper landed in a roped-off area at the corner of the car park, with SES members in bright orange uniforms providing crowd control. Ally was sitting waiting in a lolly pink convertible VW Bug to meet Santa and drive him to the stage in the garden court where his throne was waiting. Leo took his job very seriously and made a very convincing Santa Claus and the onlookers adored him.

He gave out small packets of Smith's chips, which I had obtained from the Smith's snack food company free of charge, to the crowd of eager children with the help of Joe and Fred. Then we had entertainment for everyone. A troupe of girls from the local dancing school, who were dressed as Santa's helpers, entertained the crowd with Christmas songs and dances on our new outdoor stage while Santa escaped upstairs with Ally and had tea and cake in the office. It was a very happy day and next day we got excellent media coverage much to the annoyance of the other shopping centres.

My Christmas present from Rob arrived in the form of an official letter from the managing agents. It stated that the owner of Pacific Palms Shopping Centre, Mr Robert Barclay, had recommended that I receive a salary increase and also an end of year bonus for diligence and ingenuity. I was so thrilled and could not wait to see Rob again and thank him in person. So now with my pay rise, I could afford to move and rent a unit closer to work and the beach.

A few months later, I decided to go down to Melbourne and visit Sue. I knew that she would not be herself. I had noticed our phone calls had become weird. The morphine was in control and she had faded away from reality.

The last conversation we had had ended with her saying that she had to hang up as there was one of Santa's reindeer sitting outside on her letterbox. I was so upset and I thought that if I left it any longer, she might not know me.

I only went down for a weekend but that was enough. My beautiful sister was so pale and emaciated. My heart went out to her and I knew that she was not long for this world. My dear little nieces were so brave and attended to their mother's every need. Dick was solemn and serious. No one wanted to even think about the inevitable. I took one last photo of Sue and was so sorry afterwards as she had tried to smile but the effort was too much for her. I felt terrible but I needed to have something to take back to show Mum and Dad, who tragically had been unable to visit her because of Mum's deteriorating health. Dad was beside himself as he realised that he would never see his beloved Sue again and that also he could be in danger of losing both of the women that he loved the most in the whole world.

In a few weeks' time, we received the awful news. Sue had passed away. I was crushed! We all were! I flew down immediately and in the plane, developed shingles on one side of my right breast.

At the funeral, the little Anglican church in the hills was packed and as Sue had last taught at St Margaret's School, they had their choir singing the hymns. I tried to visualise my dear little sister lying inside the coffin, from when she was the beautiful little baby I had loved to the wonderful woman she had become and whom I adored before the heinous disease had taken her away from us. Then I remembered that my nieces had requested that their mum be dressed in her favourite pink satin pyjamas as her last wish. It was so sad!

Sue, I knew, was in a better place now but Dick and Bridie and Myf were all alone. And I didn't have a little sister any more.

My only consolation was that Sue had left behind two daughters that I would always love and look upon as my own.

The death of my sister had left a permanent gap in my life and I remained depressed for a long time. Fortunately, Dick was able to look after the girls but I knew that it would not be easy. He was completely heartbroken and I felt guilty that I could not do much to help, owing to the fact that I lived so far away.

To help overcome my grief, I decided to throw myself deeper into my work and so Pacific Palms prospered due to my efforts. Rob was obviously very pleased at my results and gave the managing agents in Brisbane the sack and increased my salary. I now had a lot more responsibilities but nothing that Ally and I couldn't handle, and I started to feel better.

The first weekend I could, I went to see Mum. She was not well and I could tell that she was losing weight fast. Dad confided in me when we were alone that it was definitely the beginning of the end as the cancer had returned to her other breast and spread elsewhere.

So I decided that maybe Bridie and Myf may like to see their grandmother before she became too ill, and Dick jumped at the chance to have a change of scenery as he was still in deep mourning for Sue. So they all arrived for a short trip in the school holidays and Dick stayed with me, and the girls with Mum and Dad.

It was heart-wrenching to see Dick still pining for Sue so much and as I was going to Toastmasters on his last evening, I invited him along. He loved it and when they went back home, he joined a local group.

I was so pleased that I had been able to introduce him to something that would help take his mind off his seemingly never-ending grief.

Then out of the blue, Rob phoned me at work from Sydney and said he was arriving the next day and would I switch the hot water service on for him in his unit.

I was elated and so after work, Ally and I hurriedly decorated his unit with fresh fruit and flowers and I scattered a trail of rose petals, ending on his bed, which I knew he would love.

The following day, Rob arrived after spending a long time in America and anxiously asked me if I had received a postcard from him. He was quite upset when I said that I hadn't received it but he said that he had had a lot on his mind and that it should come soon.

It was a hot September morning when we awoke after a wonderful night making rapturous love but unfortunately, I had to rush off early as I had a meeting with the Traders Association. Rob came into the bathroom as I was showering and said that he would go for a run and would see me later at the office. I yelled out that I would leave the makings of his breakfast on the table for when he returned.

But he never did.

A mutual friend called into the office during the meeting to tell me he had seen Rob being put into an ambulance and taken to the Nambour Hospital.

I rang the hospital and they confirmed my worst nightmare. They said that he had collapsed in a nearby park with a massive heart attack when jogging and had been dead on arrival.

Then they asked me to go to their morgue to identify the body.

Suddenly my whole world had ended.

My soul mate was dead. How horrible!

He was such a fit man and I could not understand why this had happened. It was awful. I felt as if I wanted to crash my four-wheel drive on the way to the hospital and end my life as well but then I thought of Hayden. I couldn't do it and besides, I knew that Rob would not have wanted me to do such a stupid thing. I could hear his voice in my head, telling me to be strong and that he loved me, and I thought that I must be going crazy!

It was all so sudden. I had envisaged years of happiness with him, living together in absolute harmony and love until we were old. Why did this have to happen now, of all times? It wasn't fair!

My experience in the mortuary was one that I never wanted to go through again. When I kissed the face of my darling Rob, it was cold and as hard as concrete. The lips that I had known were non-responsive and like a block of ice. He had gone but I knew instantly that his body was just a shell, and that his spirit would be immortal.

He was now in heaven.

The policeman asked me to indicate the name of the body and I managed to choke out his name, with uncontrollable tears gushing out of my eyes. He was understanding but also coldly clinical.

I drove back to Pacific Palms, shaking, and Ally helped me get through one of the most dreadful days of my life.

Later, we returned to Rob's unit.

I sadly packed up all my belongings and we cleaned the place from top to bottom and Ally helped me load up my vehicle and we left.

Next day, I collected the office mail from the post office box and was shocked.

Rob's postcard from America had arrived.

I was completely shattered when I read it.

Dear Lynne,
I only want to say I love you.
I wish to share my life with you, knowing that you will be very understanding and loving.
In return, I promise you my devotion and true friendship.
Rob.

So now I knew. This was his way of proposing.

Every morning afterwards, whilst walking on the beach, Rob seemed to be with me and he spoke to me, trying to ease my pain. I didn't tell anyone of my experience as I knew they would think I was deluded. However, it was wonderful to hear his voice in my mind, comforting me. As I walked along where we had walked many times, I remembered all our conversations and I realised that I must be in touch with Rob's spirit. It was a wonderful connection and I continued to keep it to myself. It was a very private thing and Rob had always been that way about important things that had concerned us only.

However, after a few months, one morning, he said that it was time for him to go away.

I felt so sad but I had to face it. I had been privileged to have him with me for that period of time but of course, I had not wanted it to end. Then he said that he would always love me and we would be together one day, in a new life.

I fell into a relaxed state and stopped and stared out to sea and then up to the cloudless sky. It was all such a mystery, and I still wondered why Rob had been taken away from me so soon but I dared not question God's will.

I was in a state of numbness and the only thing that kept me going was my work but nothing would ever be the same again. All my friends were concerned but no one except Ally had any idea what I was going through, and I wondered if I would ever get over it.

As Christmas was coming, I had to plan a promotion that would be the top one again but somehow, my heart was not in it. However, I took the easy way out and got a stretch limousine complete with chauffeur to drive Santa into the centre. The Sunshine Coast only had two of these vehicles at that time as they were brand new and were a real novelty and our centre scooped all the publicity once again, as 'Santa Arrives in Style'.

My sadness increased when I went to visit Mum. She was like a little bag of bones and seemed to be away with the fairies, caused by the morphine in her painkillers.

Dad was beside himself with worry and we both agreed that animals were treated better than humans in these situations as she was fading away from us so fast.

After I had left, in the next hour or so, my beautiful mother, dearest Dora Pauline, had passed away peacefully in her bed.

Thank goodness that there would be no more pain for her.

But there would be no more Mum for me!

At least I knew that she would be in heaven, with Sue and Paul, and in God's loving care. It was the only consolation I had.

Dad never got over Mum's death. He aged very quickly afterwards and the only things left in his life that he enjoyed were playing bowls and doing the garden. I was glad that he was capable of looking after himself as I did not really want the responsibility of caring for him. I used to visit him every Saturday afternoon and bring chicken pies that he liked for lunch. He was like a lost soul but then, I was like one too and so we had something in common for once in our lives. It was quite amazing but we were actually starting to get close.

Hayden had just sold his carpet cleaning business and wanted to try his luck living in Perth for a year or two with some old school friends who had a travel agency and had invited him to share their house and had a job vacancy.

As Western Australia seemed so far away, I decided that this was a golden opportunity to arrange a little farewell party for him with just Dad and me.

It all went so well and after a few drinks, they both buried the hatchet and happily shook hands as they said goodbye.

Dad seemed to have finally mellowed and I could feel that he was reaching out to me, probably as I was the only one left who had a direct link to Mum and Sue. I could see that I had now become the most important person in his life.

Then one Saturday, during a pre-lunch drink, Dad decided to open up about his early life on their farm in Gulgong, New South Wales.

At nine years old, he was sent away to boarding school in Albury where the boarders were practically starved. He related how the boys would count the baked beans on their plates at breakfast and then divide them all up equally between them. It was a Spartan existence with the school making them take cold showers every day, even in the freezing winter.

Then I heard about my grandfather, whom I had never liked. He was a strict, evil man, who ruled his family with a rod of iron. At the age of fourteen, he had made Dad work like a man, from dawn till dusk, in the hot sun during the harvest, lifting and carrying sacks of wheat on his back, and was also quick to dish out corporal punishment for no good reason.

I suddenly realised that he must have broken Dad's spirit.

Perhaps Dad had been the way he had because he had the misfortune to have a violent father and a cold-hearted mother.

Also, the experience of going to war had not helped as I surmised that until my father had met my mother, he had never known real love at all.

So it made sense that he wanted her undivided love and did not want anyone or anything to come between them, except Sue, who was the 'apple of his eye' and born after the war.

I then understood why my birth had unfortunately upset the apple cart for him. I supposed Dad could not handle coming home from the war and having to share my mother's love with a baby, and I deduced he must have considered that I may not be his child as had happened with some of his comrades who were away with him. These revelations were invaluable to me and helped answer questions I had wondered about him for years. I now had answers. Dad had finally decided to confess to me why he had acted in the way he had as he had hit me, quite a lot, for no good reason as a young child when out of Mum's view.

I now understood. The pieces of the puzzle had come together at long last and I found myself actually feeling sorry for my lonely old father. He looked as though he had shrunken with age and seemed so frail and harmless now, and I realised that he was sorry for his violent actions to me, Paul and Hayden.

As I was leaving, he looked up at me with eyes that were pleading forgiveness and I gave him a hug. Then, he gave me one back and then a little peck on the cheek. I thought that I may have been repulsed but I wasn't. I was relieved and in fact, we both were.

I waved goodbye and we gave each other genuine smiles.

When walking outside to the car, a wonderful feeling engulfed me. Suddenly, a cross I had been bearing almost all of my life had been lifted from my weary shoulders.

Chapter 28

Cupid Strikes Again

On the following Monday, I went to work as usual. Ally and I were still at Pacific Palms and it was 1993, almost three years since my beloved Rob had passed away.

Even though a considerable time had elapsed, I knew that there would never be another man for me. I didn't mind in a way, because I had experienced a unique relationship that most people would never know. I had been lucky, even if our time on this Earth together had been fleeting.

I would always regard Rob as my soul mate.

My close friends Meg and Ted, of course, were always trying to match me up with someone else but had been hugely unsuccessful until one evening they invited me to have drinks at their clifftop home. They proudly introduced me to their old friend, yachting legend Jock Sturrock, who was staying with them. He was a lot older than me but I found him to be ageless in his outlook and very charming. Jock had us all in stitches, recalling their days together on the high seas. He seemed to be such a down-to-Earth person, which really appealed to me.

At the end of the party, I offered to help him walk down the steep driveway to his car as previously, he had suffered a mild stroke and needed assistance.

That was the start of Jock and I developing a much-needed friendship. We were both alone and missing our soul mates that had departed this world.

So we agreed to be just good friends but soon our relationship grew closer and we experienced a different kind of love that we both had never had.

At first, it was built on mutual respect and affection as we knew that it could never replace our previous partners but as we grew closer, it seemed right to take the next step further and have sex in our lives, which we both needed and enjoyed.

Dad liked Jock immediately and I think he was glad that I had found a new partner, which he could never do.

Ally also liked Jock and one morning as we sat down for our morning coffee at work, she asked how things were going with him. I told her of the latest development and she smiled and nodded her head in approval.

Then surprisingly, we saw Constable Keith at the office door and I immediately thought of the usual problems in the shopping centre like shoplifting or overnight break-ins.

However, I was wrong as he had come to see me about a personal matter. His usual smile had suddenly become serious and he told me to sit down.

'I'm afraid I have some bad news for you, Lynne.

'Your father was found dead this morning in the garage of his home.

'He had taken his own life by gassing himself in his car.'

I immediately froze and could not speak.

'Would you please go to the hospital morgue to identify the body as soon as possible?'

Then he handed me a note written in Dad's handwriting and some personal effects bound by a rubber band, including a diary, which the police said they had made photocopies of relevant pages. Ally was horrified and handed me the tissue box.

I unfolded the note and my silent tears flowed as I read it.

Dear Lynnie
I have contracted bowel cancer and so feel I must go.
Love
Dad xxx

It was such a shock! I didn't have any idea that my father had bowel cancer.

At the mortuary, I stood nervously outside the curtained window. It was all too much for me after my last experience there and I started getting really upset and almost hysterical.

As the curtain rolled back, I saw the attendant lift up the sheet, exposing the peaceful face of my dear father finally at rest away from all torments of his life. It reminded me of Rosebud summer holidays when I would see him enjoying floating in the water on his back with his eyes closed. He loved floating like that and for one moment, I imagined his soul floating up to heaven to join Mum.

They would both be happy now and would be with Sue and Paul.

Then the officer asked me to state the name of the deceased and after sipping some water, I managed to say my father's name.

The policeman told me that Dad's suicide had been well planned. He said that Dad had made sure that his bowling friends would discover him and not me. Then he asked me if I would like to go inside before they covered up the body and say goodbye privately. I decided to go in and they left me alone and I kissed him on the forehead. It was as cold and hard as ice, as I suspected it would be. However, he smelt very strongly of exhaust fumes and one side of his face had started to decompose. I took a last look at him and realised that I really had loved my father in the end. What a shame it had taken so long for us to finally bond. I had only just found the real him! I knew then that I would miss him from now on, more than ever.

I drove back to his house to check if it was locked. The garage door was wide open because it still smelt of exhaust fumes. I looked inside the Ford Laser where Dad had last been and then I saw one of his slippers left on the floor near the car. I rushed out of the garage and locked it and felt like vomiting.

After that, I unlocked the front door and went inside. It was immaculate and Dad had even left a note for me to return his library books. As I walked through the place, it felt as if Mum and Dad were just out and would be home any minute but of course, I really knew that they would never be coming home. They had both died in this house. How I hated it! It gave me the creeps but I knew that I would have to come back when I was ready to sell it.

I decided to take all the photo albums and framed photos of the family with me that day. There was nothing else that I wanted to take away immediately. I had earmarked some family heirloom paintings for my cousin to hand down to his sons for safe keeping on my mother's side of the family, where they belonged.

I realised my father had had real problems but at last, I could now put it all behind me.

A huge feeling of stress and anxiety from all those past years was gone. Strangely, I felt almost weightless.

I quickly gathered up all the family photos, picked up Dad's library books and locked the front door.

Before I drove away, I had a last look at the house and although feeling sad, I was thankful that I could now get on with my life without any more demons haunting me.

I had been to hell and back that day but I knew then that I was now finally at peace.

Sometime after my father's funeral, I decided to contact his doctor and find out more about him having cancer. He was very co-operative and said that as far as he knew, my father did not have anything wrong with him at all.

I told him that Dad had written in his last note to me that he believed he had bowel cancer and the doctor diplomatically advised me to draw my own conclusions.

Then I thought back as to what Constable Keith had said, and I agreed that Dad had planned his suicide very well. It all made perfect sense now. Dad had had enough of life and had been able to tie up loose ends and we had both ended up growing closer, and accepting each other, something I never dreamt would happen.

Then one day I saw something sad on TV. Fourteen years after Paul's death, there was a terrible tragedy at the Kew Cottages. A fierce fire broke out during the night in the unit that Paul had last been in. The unit had housed twenty-five young men but nine of them had lost their lives when the roof caved in. One of the little boys that I fondly remembered when Paul lived there was a Down's Syndrome child and sadly I saw his name in the paper listed with the others that had perished.

For years, I had been haunted by a guilty feeling for admitting Paul to an institution but somehow, after this horrendous event, I had now found final closure to this reoccurring nightmare as my darling Jock helped me through it as he had with Dad's passing.

After happily living together for some time, Jock and I were married privately. Apart from my deep love, Jock had my great admiration for his yachting achievements and also his many humanitarian accomplishments and accolades. He had said, 'If you set your mind on something worthwhile, then it is achievable.'

So we had three years of wonderful married bliss and fun times but then, as he suffered from angina, it worsened. He badly needed a quadrupled open-heart operation but unfortunately, it scrambled his brain and he was never the same again.

He had to be admitted to a nursing home where he eventually passed on in his early eighties. I was there at his bedside holding his hand when it happened.

It was another heartbreaking time for me.

I felt so lost, and alone, once again.

Then back at work, I was informed that the Hong Kong company that now owned Pacific Palms had it on the market and so I had to start thinking about my future. I had been employed at Pacific Palms for over six years.

It sold quickly and Ally and I were given notice. I was lucky and got a job soon afterwards at Dolphin Plaza, a neighbouring shopping centre, and stayed there until I retired. Also, Ally got a private job with an accountant and we have remained forever friends.

As the years went by, when I was considering retiring, I saw a coloured leaflet in the paper advertising a new estate at Sandy Inlet, a fishing village. It boasted a pristine beach of white sand with shells and looked beautiful in the photo and so I took a drive up to inspect it. I couldn't believe it when I actually saw it.

It seemed to be the perfect place that I was yearning for to relax and enjoy the rest of my life.

Within a matter of weeks, my house was sold and I was on my way.

I had been a bit worried the first morning when I set foot on the beach there as I didn't know a soul but as I walked along the sand with my two little white dogs, I suddenly felt in my heart that I would never be alone.

I soon made friends with some ladies from the neighbourhood and they invited me to go with them and their husbands to a Melbourne Cup Day luncheon at the local bowling club.

Although I didn't have a partner, I was quite happy just to be there; as a former Melbournian, I had always loved the first Tuesday in November.

There happened to be a spare seat next to me and as luck would have it, a very distinguished-looking gentleman asked if he could sit next to me if the seat wasn't taken.

'Hello. I'm Stirling Ferguson,' he said, as he sat down and his blue eyes twinkled. 'Are you new in town?'

'Yes,' I replied. 'I'm Lynne.'

And we immediately shook hands quite enthusiastically.

He spoke so beautifully and I wasn't surprised when he said that he was originally from Melbourne. We had so much in common and found out that we had gone to brother-and-sister private colleges there. It was an amazing coincidence.

That day was the beginning of a wonderful relationship that is still going strong. At the start, we made it clear before it got too serious that neither of us wanted to live with a partner or remarry again as we had both been living alone for a long period of time and were set in our own ways. So it suited us so well, particularly as we lived around the corner from each other. Everything just fell into place and I am sure that divine providence had something to do with it as we soon fell in love and I realised how fortunate I was to have found Stirling in such a quiet little seaside town.

Amongst other things, we enjoyed fishing from his boat or going off-road in his four-wheel drive for picnics to our favourite secluded spots up the beach or on the river bank. We both fit in so well with the laidback lifestyle of the place. Sometimes it was hard to believe that we had both spent our younger lives, living in busy Melbourne.

Meanwhile, Hayden was still living on the Sunshine Coast and had made a change from his work in travel after studying for his qualifications in a new career as a disability support worker.

He loved his new job and had a real rapport with his clients and most importantly, felt he was doing something helpful with his life.

So at long last, things had settled down and were going so well for us all.

However, some years later, I had an urgent phone call from Hayden with some shocking news. His father had suffered an unexpected heart attack. Stan had passed away alone at his home, a day or two previously. Neighbours, who usually went walking with him every morning, had made the grim discovery and called the police.

Naturally, Hayden took it badly as he had been very close to his Dad and had spent most weekends with him. I flew down and gave Hayden as much support that I could and helped organise the funeral and get all the other affairs in order.

It was a very trying time for both of us.

Not long after this, I developed a painful back problem that was increasing and my GP advised me to think of moving to a warmer climate as the winters were becoming too cold for me. But before that, he referred me to a specialist in Brisbane, who turned out to be marvellous. Not only did I have bulging discs in the lower back but skeletal scoliosis, which was undetected by the previous local specialists I had seen. My spine was tilting to the right and I had to have a full back reconstruction with titanium rods and screws inserted before I turned seventy.

It was a mammoth operation at the Wesley Hospital and when I had recovered from it, I was pain-free. It was a miracle as without the operation, I would have been confined to a wheel chair within three years' time. I was so grateful and thanked God.

As a result, I needed to be in a warm climate all year round and chose to move to a tropical paradise in Far North Queensland after selling my house. Stirling drove me up and helped me settle in but unfortunately, he felt that the humid weather would not suit him and so he decided to stay put at Sandy Inlet.

However, Hayden decided to move up there from Melbourne, which was really great.

Also, just before Covid first hit, I was able to fulfil my bucket list dream of going to the Taj Mahal in India and being photographed sitting on Princess Diana's seat.

It was unbelievable!

I now have made close friends and also Princess Daisy, my little Maltese dog, and as I live near a picturesque palm-tree-fringed beach, we love walking there.

So after many years, I still feel blessed having Stirling in my life. He flies up regularly throughout the year for our 'honeymoon' reunions.

However, I do miss him and so in his absence, one day Roger came into my life and started fulfilling my sexual needs. He is always there when I need him and never lets me down.

Stirling doesn't mind at all and when I told him about it, he said, 'Go for it, honey bun!'

Just for the record, Roger lives in my bedside drawer and so far, he has lived up to his name:

Roger the Rabbit – The Clitoral Vibrator.

So Stirling and I are very happy having the perfect arrangement, which suits us both now we are in our twilight years and we phone each other every couple of days.

Another amazing chapter of my life keeps unfolding, and so I intend to make the most of it.

THE END

Shawline Publishing Group Pty Ltd
www.shawlinepublishing.com.au

www.ingramcontent.com/pod-product-compliance
Lightning Source LLC
Chambersburg PA
CBHW012004090526
44590CB00026B/3871